The DIY Investor

Every owner of a physical copy of this edition of

The DIY Investor – Third Edition

can download the eBook for free direct from us at Harriman House,
in a format that can be read on any eReader, tablet or smartphone.

Simply head to:

ebooks.harriman-house.com/diyinvestor3ed

to get your free eBook now.

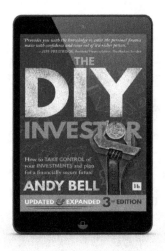

The DIY Investor

How to take control of your investments and plan for a financially secure future

Third Edition

Andy Bell

Harriman
House

HARRIMAN HOUSE LTD
3 Viceroy Court
Bedford Road
Petersfield
Hampshire
GU32 3LJ
GREAT BRITAIN
Tel: +44 (0)1730 233870
Email: enquiries@harriman-house.com
Website: harriman.house

This third edition published in Great Britain in 2021
Copyright © Andy Bell

The right of Andy Bell to be identified as the author has been asserted in accordance
with the Copyright, Design and Patents Act 1988.

Paperback ISBN: 978-0-85719-818-1
eBook ISBN: 978-0-85719-819-8

British Library Cataloguing in Publication Data

A CIP catalogue record for this book can be obtained from the British Library.

CONTENTS

ABOUT THE AUTHOR

Born in Liverpool in 1966, Andy Bell was educated at Rainford High School and then went on to study at the University of Nottingham. He graduated with a first-class degree in Mathematics in 1987 and subsequently joined a large insurance company as a trainee actuary.

Somewhat disillusioned with the financial services industry, Andy took a sabbatical in 1990, which lasted for three years on and off, to coach football and tennis (of a fashion) in America, followed by an extended period of travel and growing up.

When Andy returned to the UK, he resurrected his actuarial career and qualified as a Fellow of the Institute of Actuaries in 1993, while working at a small actuarial consultancy.

AJ Bell was established in 1995 by Andy Bell and Nicholas Littlefair in a 149-square-foot office, funded by £10,000 of personal loans. It has since grown into one of the largest investment platforms in the UK and was listed on the London Stock Exchange in December 2018. AJ Bell is now a FTSE 250 company with over £60bn of assets under administration. AJ Bell has offices in Manchester and London, employing approximately 900 staff. It looks after a wide variety of retail clients, many of them DIY investors.

AJ Bell (www.ajbell.co.uk) offers investment solutions to DIY investors as well as clients of financial advisers and other financial services companies. Its award-winning DIY investment platform is called AJ Bell Youinvest (www.youinvest.co.uk) and AJ Bell also owns the popular *Shares* magazine (www.sharesmagazine.co.uk).

Andy was ninth in *Management Today's* 2010 Britain's top 100 entrepreneurs and AJ Bell is one of only a handful of companies ever to appear in the *Sunday Times* Profit Track and Fast Track (top 100 UK private companies with the fastest-growing profits and revenues respectively) in the same year. Both Andy and the company have won numerous other business and industry awards.

Andy lives in Lancashire with his wife Tracey, their four children, a dog and an ever-growing menagerie of farmyard animals. His interests are skiing, horse racing, playing 5-a-side football, padel tennis and watching Everton FC. Andy also has a passion for refurbishing historic buildings, one of which is home to his two-Michelin-star restaurant Moor Hall (www.moorhall.com) in Aughton, West Lancashire.

Andy set up his own charitable trust in 2011 and has a number of other charitable and business interests.

PREFACE

I can't abide intellectual arrogance. I have no time for people who think they are cleverer than they are or, even worse, people who deliberately try to sound intelligent at the expense of others. Most subject matter, when explained well by someone who understands it, makes sense. So I have a simple rule in life, and that is if I don't understand something then it must be the fault of the person who has just explained it to me.

Hopefully that doesn't sound like intellectual arrogance.

So what does this have to do with DIY investing?

Well, what puts off most people from looking after their own finances is fear. A fear of the unknown. A fear of not being able to understand the subject matter. A fear that they might feel stupid.

The world of investments can appear impenetrable – full of statistics, jargon and acronyms – but being a DIY investor can be as simple or complicated as you want it to be and you *can* become a DIY investor, if you want to. And remember, if you don't understand this book, it is not your fault, it is mine.

I finished the preface in the first edition by saying that this would be the only book I would ever write. I remain firm to that stance, but one of the problems of writing a book about financial services is that it goes out of date very quickly, hence this third edition.

In the time since the first edition was published we have seen the introduction of pension freedoms, the Innovative Finance ISA, the Help to Buy ISA and the Lifetime ISA. The lifetime allowance for pension benefits has continued on its downward trend, the annual allowance for pension contributions has been cut for high earners, taxation of dividends has changed, commission payments to financial advisers have been banned and we have seen the fall-out from the Woodford affair. Oh, and we voted to leave the EU and are facing life in the shadow of a global pandemic. DIY investing never stands still.

So, who should read *The DIY Investor*, and why?

The *who* question is easy. The answer is anybody who is thinking of, or is currently, managing their own investments. Today's and tomorrow's DIY investors – a group that industry experts expect to increase in number to 7 million over the next few years.

The answer to the *why* question is to gain the knowledge, understanding and confidence you need to take control of your finances and meet your investment objectives.

The best way to grow your assets is through the stock market, which is statistically proven to have beaten returns from banks and building societies over long periods for more than a century. This book gives you the knowledge you need to be an investor in the stock market, showing you how to cut out unnecessary costs and put your money directly into the wealth-generating sectors of the economy. You will learn how to invest your money efficiently and avoid making expensive mistakes. It is designed both for beginners and existing DIY investors who want to hone their skills and fine tune their approach to investing.

This is not a *get rich quick* book, nor is it anti-establishment. Financial advisers, wealth managers and fund managers all have a vital role to play in managing investments and most do a fantastic job. But now that financial advisers have to charge explicit fees rather than commission, financial advice has become a luxury that only the wealthy can afford. For those not ready or able to work with an adviser, this book provides the help and guidance you need to get started.

I have tried to structure this book in a logical format and, where possible, explain new concepts as I introduce them, but at times I have chosen to leave the detail until the relevant chapter. If you can't wait, you can use a search engine to find an internet definition of the term or concept.

Where I refer to a tax rate or allowance, unless otherwise stated, these will be the rates applicable to the 2021/22 tax year.

There are lots of people involved in writing a book and the blame is rightly mine if it doesn't hit the spot. If it does, the credit should go to the many people who have helped me on this journey. Thanks go to my friends and family, who have been brutally honest proofreaders and to my colleagues, in particular Gareth James, Daniel Coatsworth and Laura Suter, for helping me to rearrange a random collection of thoughts and words into something resembling a book.

One thing about being a DIY investor is that you have no one to reproach but yourself. Most people find this quite liberating, but it does mean you are the one who is responsible and you need to understand what you are doing. For that reason, *DYOR* is something you will come across quite regularly on financial websites – Do Your Own Research – often accompanied by some very helpful tips. What this politely means is I am happy to help, but I accept no liability and you can't sue me.

Being a DIY investor is not hard but it does require a measure of effort and engagement on your part. All you need is a computer, an internet connection, your bank card and the time it takes to read the parts of this book relevant to what you want to achieve.

So welcome to the world of DIY investing. There are ups and downs, but it can also deliver real financial rewards. I hope you enjoy reading this book and don't forget: I am here to help, but DYOR.

Andy Bell

PART ONE

WHAT BEING A DIY INVESTOR IS ALL ABOUT

1

INTRODUCING DIY INVESTING

Why be a DIY investor?

"Because nobody cares as much about my money as I do." This quote came out of a survey that AJ Bell commissioned to understand why people had chosen to become a DIY investor. It is all well and good thinking or saying it, but action is required.

A life event can often be the trigger for someone reviewing and taking control of their investments. The life event may be a new job, redundancy, retirement, marriage, divorce, inheritance, having a child, a child going to university and the list goes on. It is clear that the COVID-19 pandemic has been one such life event, which has driven a noticeable increase in the number of DIY customers.

The lack of engagement many people have with their investments never ceases to amaze me. Many of us spend hours scouring the internet to save a few quid on a new phone, eat at restaurants we otherwise wouldn't be seen dead in to take advantage of a coupon discount scheme, or buy three items for the price of two when we only need one.

That is human nature – everyone likes a bargain. But translate that into far bigger financial decisions and most people simply haven't got a clue. Ask someone how much they have in their ISA (individual savings account) or pension, what charges they pay, what they are invested in, how much they need to retire, or even what interest rate they're getting on their cash savings account and a look of quizzical bemusement takes over.

The fact that you are reading this book means you probably don't fit into this category or, if you do, you are desperate to break free. Learning how to become a DIY investor enables you to set basic goals and implement a simple strategy to achieve them. You will strip out a whole layer of charges that will free up your investments to grow quicker and hit your desired targets sooner than would otherwise be the case.

I am often asked, "What is the minimum amount of money I need to become a DIY investor?" My reply is always the same, after checking for eavesdroppers to avoid embarrassment. "It is not about size, it is about your state of mind." There is a DIY solution for everyone, irrespective of how much you want to invest. But you do need a willingness to take control of your investments and the ability to dedicate at least a small amount of time.

Follow the strategies, ideas and tips set out in this book and you will learn how to create the sort of portfolio that you would get from a professional adviser, without paying the charges.

What you won't get from this book are share tips, instructions on how to spot good or bad companies, or a guide to equity valuation metrics. There is plenty of other material available out there that goes into these specific areas.

Why everyone should invest – DIY or otherwise

However you choose to invest for your future, the necessity of doing so is an imperative for us all. The government has made no secret of the fact that it expects us to provide for ourselves, both before and during retirement.

For instance, the government has made changes to the system so that employees are automatically enrolled in pension schemes. What's more, the age at which we'll all get our state pension is steadily increasing and there's even been talk of the government considering the possibility of raising the age to 70 years old. Therefore, it seems inevitable that everyone must do more to save for their future, as the government will not provide enough to provide you with a comfortable retirement.

Providing for your children could be one of your investment objectives, and this could be for a number of reasons: to pay for their school fees, university fees, help with their first house or just buy them their first car. Providing for private school fees is expensive enough, but we have also seen university fees triple in recent years, and with graduates coming out of university with an average debt of £50,000, it is understandable parents might want to help out with that.

Or your primary goal may be more focused around your own retirement.

Retirement ages are increasing and anyone in their early thirties today will not get their state pension until the age of 68 at the earliest. State pension age is being linked to how long we live and as life spans increase, so the day you will get your pension recedes further into the future.

I attended an actuarial conference a few years ago and the heading of one session was, 'Immortality is no longer a pipe dream'. While the speaker may have been stretching the point, the heading succinctly highlights the direction of travel. Increasing longevity means longer in retirement, which may sound great but it also makes saving for your retirement a real uphill battle.

Just how much longer everyone is living can be hard to digest – the statistics are phenomenal. Back in 1952, only 300 people in the UK had made it to the age of 100. By 2018, the number of centenarians living in the UK had risen to 13,170, according to the Office for National Statistics (ONS).

And every new generation seems to be living longer than the last. A baby boy born in 2018 is expected to live until 88; and a baby girl to 90. These are average figures, so many could live longer. Particularly because they include those who will become overweight, smokers, heavy drinkers and those with long-term health conditions, which brings the average down. You may not believe it, and you may not even want to believe it, but these days if you are of above-average health you are in with a decent shot of making it to 100.

This means if you want to retire aged 60 then unless you have got a final salary, or defined benefit pension, you will have to put away a small fortune to pay the bills for a retirement that could run into three, four or even five decades.

It is clear doing nothing is not an option, so everyone needs to invest for the future in some way.

But that doesn't mean you have to take on absolutely everything yourself. If you don't understand something, or you are involved in a complicated situation, don't be afraid to ask for help. Being a DIY investor means making your own financial decisions, but it doesn't mean you are an expert at everything.

There are times in your life when you have to accept that someone else could provide the best solution to a problem. This applies to calling in a tradesman to fix a botched home repair job or getting a mechanic to overhaul your car after your quick fix turned into a big mess.

It also applies to managing your money, particularly in the complicated world of tax. Inheritance tax is a classic example of where it can pay to seek advice from an expert. Divorce is another situation where you may need the help of a financial adviser in trying to separate your assets.

What does being a DIY investor entail?

Being a DIY investor can involve as much or as little effort on your part as you want it to. You could set up a well-researched, low-maintenance investment portfolio from scratch in less than an hour, which only needs an hour or two every six months or so to review it. Or you can create a more complex portfolio that may require daily or weekly monitoring.

The choice is yours, but please don't dive in at the deep end. Read this book and then ask yourself the question, "Am I a DIY investor?" If the answer is yes, you will likely be particularly interested in one or more investment styles and strategies highlighted in later chapters and you are ready to go. If the answer is no, then you need to seriously consider appointing a financial adviser.

You may have accumulated one or more old pensions or savings policies. The policy documents may be getting dusty in your filing cabinet and at some stage, as part of this process, you will have to dust these down and consider consolidating them all into one pension you can manage. This will give your portfolio a decent kick-start, but more on this later.

Being a DIY investor does require some commitment on your part. Because you are not paying for advice, you are buying on a *caveat emptor*, or buyer beware, basis. This means that you will be the person responsible if things go wrong. For example, if you make a mistake and buy a share or fund that you thought was something entirely different, or if you misunderstand a tax planning strategy, then you will have no one to blame but yourself. That might seem scary to start with, but over time you will build more confidence with this – and you'll learn from any small mistakes you make along the way.

The extent to which you should engage as a DIY investor should reflect the person you are. If you are someone who finds numbers particularly difficult to grasp then don't worry, just keep it simple. Buy a few different multi-asset funds and you will get the hang of it.

You also need to have the discipline to review your investments at least once a year and preferably twice a year, to make sure they are performing as they should. A few carefully considered Google alerts can keep you abreast of any key changes to your investments in the interim.

The skills and commitment you need will also depend on the type of investor that you intend to be. If you are going to adopt a long-term buy-and-hold strategy, you may need no more than a couple of hours a year to review your portfolio.

That said, once everything is set up, checking your investments online is so straightforward that most people find themselves regularly looking to see how their investments are faring anyway. Most investment platforms now have mobile phone applications, which you may find compulsive. There's a careful balance here, as you don't want to be too hands-off but you also don't want to be checking it so often you become obsessed with every small rise and fall in your portfolio. When we listed AJ Bell on the London Stock Exchange in December 2018, I made a commitment to myself that I wouldn't obsess over the share price. 'A sneaky peak, once a week' at the share price is all I allow myself. This is a sensible rule of thumb for how often you should look at your portfolio in between more detailed reviews.

Investment platforms

An investment platform is an internet-based service that offers the DIY investor at least three types of account:

1. self-invested personal pension, or SIPP

2. individual savings account, or ISA

3. dealing account

These are offered through an overarching account, accessed by a single login.

The platform you choose will be where you carry out all your investing, so choosing the right one with the most suitable charging structure, appropriate choice of investments and useful investor tools is very important.

The functionality that today's investment platforms offer means it has never been easier to be a DIY investor. It is no exaggeration to say that the internet has genuinely revolutionised the process of investing, in particular DIY investing.

Investment platforms today give you online access to real-time dealing, along with data and information that only a decade or so ago were exclusive to professional advisers and fund managers. There's lots more detail on what to look for when picking your platform in Chapter 19.

Different types of investment accounts

Efficient DIY investing involves using the right type of account – sometimes referred to as a product, tax wrapper or savings vehicle – at the right time.

The two main tax-efficient products you will see in this book are a SIPP, which stands for self-invested personal pension, and an ISA, which stands for individual savings account. There are now various different types of ISA, which I highlight below and explain in more detail in later chapters.

As well as a SIPP and an ISA, you will most likely need a dealing account for any investments that fall outside these two accounts.

The SIPP is a personal pension with the flexibility to invest in a wide range of investments. It is a very tax-efficient, long-term savings vehicle that allows you to save relatively large amounts of money each year and benefit from tax relief on your contributions. The downside is that currently you can't normally access the money in your SIPP until the age of 55, with this minimum age rising to 57 for most savers from 6 April 2028.

For their part, ISAs have over recent years become quite complex, with a variety of different ISA types now available.

The key ISA types that we cover in this book are:

The old faithful:

- Cash ISA

- Stocks and Shares ISA

And the variants of the above:

- Junior ISA (JISA)

- Innovative Finance ISA

And finally the hybrid between a pension and an ISA:

- Lifetime ISA

Each type of ISA is designed to meet a slightly different need and is therefore subject to different rules.

Different types of investments

As a DIY investor you should only invest in assets you fully understand. This book devotes a chapter to each of the main different types of asset you will come across. These are:

- quoted equities, which are shares in companies listed on a recognised stock exchange
- investment funds such as unit trusts and open-ended investment companies (OEICs)
- exchange-traded (or tracker) funds
- investment trusts
- corporate and government bonds
- non-mainstream assets for the more adventurous DIY investor.

Don't worry if this is the first time you have heard some of this jargon and these asset names. As far as the DIY investor is concerned, the bits you need to understand are straightforward and I explain all of this later in the book.

In Chapter 17 you will find an explanation of how to blend these different assets into a portfolio that is suited to your own attitude to risk.

How to save money on charges

There are a number of ways to save on charges and I will look at them in more detail in later chapters. First, by not having an adviser you have an immediate saving, but you don't have the benefit of their time and expertise.

Buying funds through a DIY investment platform also means you may well be able to get access to lower charges than the fund manager would impose if you went to them direct.

By funds, what I mean is a unit trust or OEIC. For this purpose they are interchangeable, and I will refer to them as funds. They do not include investment trusts and if I am referring to a tracker fund or exchange-traded fund then I will make the reference explicit. All will become clearer later in this book.

As well as shopping around for the best value investment platform, you can save money by thinking about how you invest and what you invest in. There are various types of DIY investors, ranging from those who adopt a long-term buy-and-hold strategy, to day-traders – the people who sit in front of a screen buying and selling different investments all day long.

Buying and selling investments frequently can be expensive, as you will incur charges each time you make a purchase or sale, stamp duty on purchases and also suffer the spread cost, which is the difference between the buying and the selling price of an investment. So, the less often you deal the less you pay in charges.

If you buy funds you will incur a management fee – a charge imposed by the fund manager for managing your money. You will need to understand the main types of charges so that you can compare funds.

You can minimise these management charges by buying low-cost funds, such as tracker funds, which aim to just replicate the performance of an index and so you don't need to pay the costs of a fund manager to look after your money.

You can avoid management fees altogether if you buy shares directly yourself. Even if you are a novice investor you can put together a portfolio of big defensive shares that pay healthy dividends and just sit on them. It may not be a very sophisticated strategy and the dividends aren't guaranteed to always be paid, but it is one that can be quite cost-effective and plenty of experienced investors do it.

These big dividend paying shares may underperform a rising market and outperform a falling market, but whatever the weather they should still generate some dividends. An alternative strategy, along similar lines, is to find out what the popular fund managers are holding in their funds and replicate their key holdings.

One advantage of being a DIY investor can be highlighted by imagining both you and a professional fund manager get advance notice of an impending stock market crash. You are in a position to convert your holdings to cash in an instant. The fund can't because its holdings would be too large to offload quickly without causing its own market crash. The DIY investor can be nimble and fleet of foot.

You may think fund management charges look pretty tiny, so why should you be bothered about them? The simple answer is that, over a long period, small differences in charges can make a massive difference to the size of your investment pot.

Over a 30-year timeline, if you're paying in £5,000 a year, a 0.5% per year difference in charges will mean the difference between a pension fund of £505,365 and £459,946, if we assume 7% a year growth after charges. That is a total of more than £45,419 lost just by investing with an annual charge 0.5% higher. This situation is summarised in Table 1.1.

Table 1.1: Fund management charges

	7% per annum return after charges	If additional 0.5% per annum charges are incurred
Return after 30 years on £5,000-a-year contribution	£505,365	£459,946

Save money on tax

Tax planning is as important to effective saving as slashing the costs of investing and choosing the right investments. Yes, that's right – *this is just as important as choosing what assets you are going to invest in.*

Tax relief on pension contributions can be as high as 45%, in which case it would cost just £5,500 to credit £10,000 into your SIPP. Also for SIPPs, you can withdraw a quarter of your fund as tax-free cash and money held within your SIPP grows mostly tax-free and in many situations is outside your estate for inheritance tax purposes.

ISA tax privileges are also valuable, and come with the added advantage that you can access your money when you want, although some restrictions apply to the newer breed of ISA.

And when it comes to withdrawing your money as income at retirement, carefully planned use of both growth and income investments across a SIPP, ISA and dealing account, possibly split between you and your spouse or partner, can dramatically minimise your tax bill. Details on the tax treatment of different asset classes and the tax privileges of different products are covered in their respective chapters.

The above is just a flavour of some of the issues I cover in later chapters.

If none of what I have said floats your boat then it is eBay for the book and to unbiased.co.uk to hunt out a financial adviser. But if I have whetted your appetite for more information, then it's on to Chapter 2 to understand how to set your investment objectives.

2

SETTING YOUR INVESTMENT OBJECTIVES

It is impossible to invest effectively without a clear understanding of your investment objectives. Once you have clarity on why you're investing, making investment decisions becomes a lot easier.

For many people, putting away as much as they can afford is their investment objective. Saying "I will save as much as I can" is certainly better than doing nothing, but it is like going for a drive without having decided on your final destination. You will have a far greater chance of getting where you want to be if you know where you are going from the start.

Creating a realistic set of investment objectives can be difficult, so it is fine to start with a broad objective and then work on it to turn it into a more specific goal.

As with all good objectives, your investment goals should be achievable and measurable. Owning your favourite football club, for example, is unlikely to be a realistic or a sensible investment objective for most people. Paying off your mortgage by the age of 50 or saving for your child's university fees, on the other hand, may well be.

You need to be able to measure progress towards these objectives and have a half-decent chance of achieving them. Most objectives will be set in a time frame, though you shouldn't get too worried if you don't meet your milestones on time.

When quantifying the pot of money you want to achieve in the future as an objective, don't forget the impact of inflation. This means you need to factor in that prices will rise in the future, for example, saving £10,000 in today's money will not buy you the same in ten, 15 or more years' time when you've achieved that goal. The Bank of England has a handy inflation calculator that will help you to work out by how much you might need to increase your target pot of money.

Visualising your investment objectives

You may think this sounds like psychobabble, but visualising what you are trying to achieve is the first step to achieving it. Visualising an objective makes it more vivid in your mind, making you more attached to the idea of turning it into reality. As a DIY investor there is nobody to encourage you along the way, so you need to remain motivated if you are to achieve your objectives.

The examples of objectives set out in the box below will hopefully get your mental juices flowing. There are no rights or wrongs when setting investment objectives – they are unique to you and your family. Also, they will inevitably change over time as your circumstances change and should be reviewed at least once a year.

Ideas for your investment objectives

- Repay my mortgage by 2040.
- Retire at the age of 65 with a fund to provide a £20,000-a-year income, in today's money.
- Provide an immediate income of £10,000 a year, with the additional prospect of future capital and income growth.

- Accumulate enough to fund a house deposit for my only child in ten years' time.

- Achieve an investment return of 5% a year greater than the rate available on cash deposits, after charges, while retaining reasonable access to my capital.

- Save enough money to pay for a round-the-world cruise at retirement.

I find it useful to start with a blank sheet of paper and draw a timeline. Break it into five- or ten-yearly intervals, and focus on when you think you will reach key milestones. These key milestones could be leaving university, getting married, buying your first home, having children, seeing your children through university, or retiring.

Think how you would like to be able to structure your finances to be able to respond to these events.

You may feel self-conscious at first, but seeing your words written on a piece of paper will help you untangle in your mind what your investment objectives really are. I mentioned earlier the importance of keeping these objectives under regular review. You may be promoted or find a new job paying a far higher salary, take on a big mortgage, inherit some money, get divorced or find your family increasing in size when you weren't expecting it, so you need to update your objectives at times like these to reflect these changed circumstances.

At the highest level, investment objectives normally focus on providing income or capital over a period of time or at a specific date. You may have other objectives, such as minimising tax, but this should never be an objective in isolation. You may have an overriding objective that your money should be accessible at all times or at reasonably short notice.

If you do find yourself struggling to identify your investment objectives and it really is just a case of investing as much as you can afford, then simply try to clarify two things – the time frame of your investment and whether you are looking for income and/or capital growth.

Most people hate budgeting. However, you need to do this as part of setting your objectives because if you don't know what your family income and expenditure is, you won't know how much spare cash you will have. This book is about DIY investing and not about the wider issue of family finances. Making a few quick calculations in a spreadsheet will suffice to determine how much 'available money' you have to invest.

The trick is, don't be too ambitious – invest or save only what you can realistically afford. If not, you may find yourself having to rethink your investments six months down the line so you can meet your everyday living costs.

If the time horizon within which you need access to your capital is less than three or maybe even five years, then I would suggest that DIY investing is possibly not the right solution for you. You probably need to be saving in cash-type products, such as bank or building society accounts or national savings.

Short-, medium- and long-term objectives

DIY investing is suitable for meeting medium- to long-term objectives. Most people have a blend of short-, medium- and long-term objectives. It is important to prioritise these, although it is never easy. A new car in three years or repay the mortgage in 15 years?

Most will choose the former and psychologists have described this human trait as *hyperbolic discounting*. It's the hard-wired tendency to place a far greater value on something that will be received in the near future, such as a holiday, than something in the distance, such as a pension, even if the thing further away in time is far more valuable.

Overcoming this desire for immediate gratification is incredibly hard, with the unfortunate consequence that most people only realise they need to start saving for their retirement when it is going to cost them far more to do so, as Table 2.1 demonstrates.

Fixing objectives in the context of retirement can be particularly difficult because of the shock many people experience when they realise just how much of their salary they will need to save to achieve the retirement income they expect. And the longer you leave it, the more you have to pay to get there.

Table 2.1: Proportion of salary someone earning £50,000 per year needs to pay into a pension to provide an income of 50% of salary from age 65

Age	Pension contribution
25	14%
35	23%
45	40%
55	95.50%

As Table 2.1 shows, the later you leave it to start saving for retirement, the more expensive it gets. This is not surprising, given the 55-year-old in this example is hoping to save for a retirement in just ten years that could last 30 or 40 years.

Increased life expectancy is of course a fantastic development for society, but it is making retirement planning incredibly expensive. The princely sum of £100,000 will give a male 65-year-old an inflation-linked annuity of almost £3,000 a year. Do without inflation protection and you could get just over £5,000 a year.

Fortunately you don't have to buy an annuity anymore and you can keep your money invested and choose how much you drawdown from your pension each year; but there are of course no guarantees that your chosen level of pension will be sustainable throughout your retirement.

But don't get put off by the magnitude of the challenge of saving for retirement. Burying your head in the sand is not an option, and the sooner you start, the longer your pension fund will benefit from compounding growth, the eighth wonder of the world according to Albert Einstein. And remember, most people find their earnings increase as they get older, so if you are only paying a fraction of what you need to, at least you are making a start.

There are a number of pension calculators on the internet that will work out how much you need to save to deliver a set income in retirement. These calculators may give your results in real terms, meaning they take into account inflation between now and your retirement. They may also factor in the tax relief you get on your savings.

Try www.aviva-pensioncalculator.co.uk to see whether your retirement planning is on course.

How long-term factors can impact your objectives

I mentioned the impact of inflation earlier. As a rule of thumb, if inflation is running at 3% per annum, then £100 today is worth £75 in ten years and £55 in 20 years. If inflation is at 5% per annum, these figures reduce to £61 and £38 respectively.

Planning for income in retirement is even more difficult, as you not only have to factor in the impact of inflation – often over a very long time – but you also need a rough idea of how many years you are going to live.

Unless you are one of the lucky ones in a final salary scheme, or are not put off by the prohibitive cost of buying an annuity, the chances are you will enter retirement with a pot of money and the challenge of investing this to provide a long-term income in retirement. The good news is DIY investing is the perfect way to meet this challenge.

Avoiding emotional investing

Before we turn to understanding the detail of the tax wrappers and investments you will encounter, I would just like to comment on the psychology of investing. It is important to recognise that you will need to adopt a dispassionate and emotionless attitude if you are to become a successful DIY investor.

If you are an incessant worrier, your life is an emotional roller-coaster ride, or even if you find yourself watching poker on TV when you should be asleep, you will need to take a moment to sanity-check any decision to become a DIY investor.

Understanding the way your brain is programmed to react to investment situations can prevent you from having expensive knee-jerk reactions. This is particularly important for DIY investors who do not have an adviser to guide them when investment markets are volatile.

Human beings are psychologically programmed to be bad at investing. Buying at the top of the market or selling at the bottom are two classic mistakes inexperienced investors make.

Psychologists have carried out research that shows we tend to overreact when markets move significantly. When our investments rise in value we can be overcome with a feeling of euphoria and a sense of invincibility – when they fall we become stressed, fearful and wracked with regret.

The truth is, you should only ever decide whether to buy or sell an asset on your assessment of the basic fundamentals. As the well-known regulatory disclaimer goes, past performance is not a guide to future performance. One could argue that this is nonsense, because it is like saying the fact that Real Madrid have been at or near the top of European football for the past decade is no guide to their future performance, when it clearly is.

Past performance continues to be one of the most commonly used benchmarks by professional advisers when deciding where to invest, despite the warnings. But the principle behind the regulatory warning is both clear and sensible: don't follow performance graphs blindly.

Here are some methods you can employ to take the emotion out of investing.

Strategies for taking the emotion out of investing

- **Pound-cost averaging**. It sounds complicated and technical, but this is one of the simplest ways of spreading risk and smoothing the volatility of investment markets. The key point about pound-cost averaging is that you invest small amounts on a regular basis, for example £100 a month. So, when prices are high your monthly investment will buy fewer shares or units, but when prices are low your investment buys more shares or units. The cost of your investments is averaged in this way, hence pound-cost averaging.

- **Diversification.** Different types of assets tend to rise and fall in value at different times in the market cycle. By diversifying your portfolio across different geographies, asset classes and even across different sectors within an asset class, you can dampen much of the market's volatility in your portfolio.

- **Use fund managers.** While you still need to choose a fund manager, this is a lot easier and less risky than choosing individual shares. You are leaving the big decisions to them and paying them for taking the pressure off you.

- **Use tracker funds.** A bit like using a fund manager but without really worrying who the fund manager is, other than making sure they are good value for money. This option means you don't need to pick individual shares, you just need to choose the index to track and the fund with which to track it, but thereafter you can put your feet up and leave the fund to grow, hopefully without too much interference.

- **Use model portfolios or 'all-in-one' funds.** Many DIY investment platforms now offer a guided investment or model portfolio option. This is a basket of investments that constitutes a ready-made portfolio of assets – typically actively managed funds, but it may extend to tracker funds chosen by the investment platform or a firm they appoint. Model portfolios look and feel like recommendations from professional financial advisers, but they are not. They are generic recommendations offered without assessing whether they are suitable for your circumstances.

- **Control your emotions.** As a DIY investor you will need discipline and cannot afford to let emotion get in the way. If you want to become a real DIY investor, you have to be prepared to take some losses. But the flip side of this is that selling all your holdings as soon as you suffer a loss can often be the worst thing to do.

Investment objectives, appetite for risk and investment strategy

Your objectives are only one part of the investment equation. You try to achieve these objectives by implementing an investment strategy. Any investment strategy needs to be set in the context of an appetite for risk – how much risk are you willing to take to achieve your objectives?

People often conflate these three concepts – investment objectives, appetite for risk and investment strategy – but it is important to keep them separate. Think of your investment objectives as the destination, your investment strategy as the route you have chosen to get there and your risk appetite as how fast you are willing to drive!

We cover risk appetite in Chapter 17 and as for investment strategy, well that is pretty much the rest of the book. It is all about what you invest in to achieve your goals.

PART TWO

THE DIY INVESTOR'S TOOLKIT
– THE PRODUCTS

3

THE ISA –
INDIVIDUAL SAVINGS ACCOUNT

An individual savings account (ISA) is the entry level investment account and tax wrapper. It gives you the ability to invest in the stock market or to keep your money in cash in a tax-efficient way. All investment income is tax-free and there is no tax to pay on capital gains.

ISAs have become a political hot potato over recent years, being used to underpin various government initiatives, such as helping the younger generation to get on to the housing ladder, and in support of riskier areas of the finance sector, such as peer-to-peer lending and crowd funding.

While the proliferation of different types of ISA means the market isn't quite as simple as it used to be, each individual product is still relatively straightforward and easy enough to understand. The challenge comes when you try to decide which type of ISA to go for – there are five different types. Also, with the advent of the Lifetime ISA, introduced in April 2017, deciding whether to save for your retirement using a pension or an ISA has become even trickier.

The tax efficiency and easy access to your money offered by ISAs means they can be used for both short- and medium-term saving and can also sensibly form part of a DIY investor's longer-term retirement strategy.

You have an annual ISA allowance, which is the amount of money you can subscribe, i.e. pay in, each tax year. ISA allowances operate on a *use it or lose it* basis. If you haven't used your full allowance by 5 April in any tax year, it is lost forever.

The annual adult ISA allowance is £20,000 for the 2021/22 tax year. This can be spread over the different types of ISA – though note that some types of ISA impose a lower allowance.

Also, there is a lower ISA allowance of £9,000 in the 21/22 tax year for Junior ISAs, which I cover in more detail later in this chapter.

For a number of years, the Junior ISA allowance went up in line with inflation each April, but this is not guaranteed and, with the allowance more than doubling in 2020/21, I'm not expecting these inflationary increases to continue. The allowances for other ISAs have been stable for a number of years now. You can pay into an adult ISA with a different provider each year, but *you are only allowed to pay into one of each type of ISA in any one tax year*.

Just to be clear, investment returns such as interest, dividends or capital gains from investments held within an ISA do not count towards your annual ISA allowance.

Where your ISA holds cash, interest is paid to your ISA gross, i.e. without any deduction of tax. Where your ISA holds equities or funds, then there is no tax to pay on any income or dividends paid into your ISA.

Another advantage introduced in recent years is that if you die, your spouse can effectively inherit your ISA – on your death they become entitled to an additional subscription allowance equal to the value of your ISA. While the value of your ISA still falls within your estate for inheritance tax purposes, it can be transferred into an ISA in your spouse's name, thereby retaining the tax advantages, without affecting your surviving spouse's annual ISA allowance.

If, like me, you dread filling in your tax return, then one of the advantages of an ISA is that the taxman isn't interested in your ISA investments and details do not need to be supplied as part of your self-assessment.

I have set out below a brief summary of each of the different types of ISA.

Main types of ISA

There are five main types of ISA:

1. Cash ISA

A Cash ISA does what it says on the tin; you can only hold cash in this account. This typically will be with a high-street bank or building society. A Cash ISA is most likely to be appropriate if you are investing over the short term or are very cautious and don't fancy the risks that investing in the stock market brings.

If you are 16 or over, you can pay some or all of your ISA allowance into a Cash ISA.

Watch out for Cash ISA providers that lure you in with a table-topping rate, only to slash it to almost zero 12 months after you give them your money. Many of the biggest providers pay derisory rates of interest to existing customers after the introductory rate has expired, so it usually pays to shop around for the best deals and keep transferring your Cash ISA every year.

You will come across two terms in relation to a Cash ISA that are worth a brief explanation. The first is the AER, which stands for annual equivalent rate. The second is the gross rate.

The AER is the rate you want to be most concerned with, as this is the true annual return you will get from your Cash ISA. It takes account of the rate paid throughout the year, the frequency of interest payments and compound interest, meaning that if you get interest paid monthly, this interest will earn interest. A Cash ISA with an AER of 1.3% will return interest of £13 after a year on a £1,000 investment into a Cash ISA.

The gross rate is the interest rate payable at the outset, including any initial bonuses. It will make no allowance for the frequency of interest payments or compound interest.

A Cash ISA advertised with a gross rate of 1.3% will return a lesser amount if, for example, the actual rate paid drops to, say, 0.8% after a three-month introductory bonus. Only ever use the AER when comparing Cash ISA rates.

There is an argument that since the introduction of the personal savings allowance – which means basic-rate taxpayers can receive up to £1,000 interest per year tax-free (higher rate taxpayers can receive £500, additional rate taxpayers nil) – the gloss has come off Cash ISAs.

However, interest earned in your Cash ISA is always tax-free, so that leaves your personal savings allowance to be used elsewhere.

2. Stocks and Shares ISA

You can hold cash, shares, funds and bonds in a Stocks and Shares ISA. Many providers will give you access to a wide range of funds, investment trusts, government and corporate bonds and quoted shares. This is likely to be of interest if you are a longer-term investor who is willing to accept some risk to your capital.

If you are 18 or over, you can pay some or all of your ISA allowance of £20,000 into a Stocks and Shares ISA.

Stocks and Shares ISA – qualifying investments

The following asset types can all be held in a Stocks and Shares ISA:

- Shares, corporate bonds, government securities, investment trusts and exchange-traded funds listed on a recognised stock exchange, including the Alternative Investment Market (AIM). You can of course also hold cash.

- Unit trusts and OEICs – these are more simply known as funds.

These different types of asset are explained in detail in later chapters.

3. Lifetime ISA

Launched in April 2017, you can open a Lifetime ISA if you are aged between 18 and 39, and once opened you can pay into it until the day before you hit 50. The maximum amount you can pay in is £4,000 a year, which counts as part of your overall ISA allowance of £20,000 in the 2021/22 tax year.

The government will top up what you pay with a 25% bonus – this bonus is paid into your Lifetime ISA. So, if you pay the maximum £4,000 into your Lifetime ISA in a given tax year, you will receive a £1,000 bonus. The bonus on your payments will be added into your Lifetime ISA monthly in line with your ISA subscriptions.

The primary purposes of a Lifetime ISA are to help you save up for your first home and/or fund your retirement.

You can withdraw money at any time to help fund a deposit on your first home worth up to £450,000. The property must be in the UK and subject to a mortgage when you buy it, and you can't have owned any other property before – even a share in one.

If you don't buy your first property with the funds in the Lifetime ISA, you must wait until you turn 60 before accessing the funds. Any withdrawals before this date will normally incur a 25% penalty of the amount withdrawn. This penalty is designed to claw back the government bonus, for inappropriate usage of the ISA.

Supporters argue that the Lifetime ISA is a turbo-charged version of the Help to Buy ISA and a clever way of encouraging people to save – either for a first home or retirement. Critics argue it is an experiment designed to gauge the impact of removing higher rate tax relief on pension contributions.

Nevertheless, putting aside any future increases to the £4,000 annual Lifetime ISA allowance and ignoring any investment returns, you can pay up to £128,000 in subscriptions over a lifetime, which will be topped up with a £32,000 government bonus. This is a healthy deposit on a first home, or solid base amount on which to retire.

There are two other types of ISA, neither of which can be described as mainstream, but which are included here for completeness.

4. Help to Buy ISA

The Help to Buy ISA was the government's first attempt to use ISAs to help first-time buyers. The introduction of the Lifetime ISA means that it hasn't been possible to open a Help to Buy ISA since 30 November 2019.

If you've already opened a Help to Buy ISA you can continue making monthly payments of up to £200. These subscriptions don't count towards your annual ISA allowance. Over your lifetime the total subscriptions paid in, including the maximum initial payment of £1,000 that was allowed, cannot exceed £12,000.

Similar to the Lifetime ISA, there is an incentive of a 25% government bonus added to the amount you pay in to a Help to Buy ISA. The maximum bonus available is £3,000 and the bonus is only paid if your Help to Buy ISA is worth more than £1,600.

While for a Lifetime ISA the government bonus is added shortly after you pay your subscription, the Help to Buy ISA bonus is only paid when you buy your first home in the UK. Further, this bonus is only paid if your first home costs £250,000 or less (£450,000 if the house is in London).

You can only invest your Help to Buy ISA in cash – stocks and shares are not permitted.

Also, you can't contribute into a Cash ISA and a Help to Buy ISA in the same tax year. If you do choose to pay into a Help to Buy ISA then you need to transfer money you've paid into your Cash ISA for that tax year into your Help to Buy ISA (maximum of £1,200), or into a Stocks and Shares ISA, Innovative Finance ISA or non-ISA account.

So, while you can pay £160,000, including government bonuses, into a Lifetime ISA, the equivalent amount that can be used in a Help to Buy ISA is £16,000. That is quite a difference and one of the main reasons why the Help to Buy ISA is being retired in favour of the Lifetime ISA.

5. Innovative Finance ISA

The Innovative Finance ISA is designed to invest in peer-to-peer (P2P) loans, which are loans you give to other people or businesses via P2P or crowdfunding platforms, in return for a set rate of interest. P2P loans and crowdfunding split opinions. While advocates for these ISAs will still argue that they're a great way of cutting out the middlemen (i.e. the banks), I've long felt they were an accident waiting to happen. Sadly, reports of savers struggling to withdraw funds from some platforms, among a range of other issues, appear to be bearing me out.

If you are 18 or over you can make payments into an Innovative Finance ISA and these count towards the normal ISA allowance of £20,000 for the 2021/22 tax year.

Please treat these products with a lot of caution and carry out plenty of research before committing funds.

When I said there are five types of ISA, what I really meant was there are six. Actually, while writing this book I asked a number of people in the industry how many types of ISA there are and the answers ranged from four to eight. That in itself is a little worrying.

The last type of ISA I look at here is the Junior ISA.

Junior ISA

This is really no more than a kiddie's version of the Cash ISA and the Stocks and Shares ISA. It is available to hold cash and/or investments for children under the age of 18. The maximum amount you can pay into a Junior ISA is £9,000 in the 2021/22 tax year.

In the normal course of events, funds cannot be withdrawn from a Junior ISA. A child can take control of their Junior ISA from the age of 16 and it automatically converts into a full ISA – either a Cash ISA or a Stocks and Shares ISA – when the child turns 18.

Junior ISAs are a great way for parents and grandparents to fund university fees, the cost of a car or even the deposit on a house for the next generation.

Junior ISAs replaced Child Trust Funds, which ceased being offered to those born on or after 3 January 2011. A Junior ISA can be opened for anyone under the age of 18 who was born before September 2002 or on or after 3 January 2011. Children born between these dates were originally forced to save in Child Trust Funds. Money can now be transferred from a Child Trust Fund into a Junior ISA as the latter is now the investment product of choice for children.

You can establish a Junior ISA for a child as long as you have parental responsibility for them. The child must be resident in the UK.

Special transitional ISA allowance rules apply as children move from the Junior ISA regime into the adult ISA regime as they reach 16, 17 and then 18. See the footnote to the ISA comparison table at the end of this chapter for more information.

Junior ISAs and inheritance tax

If a parent, grandparent or indeed anyone else pays a subscription into a Junior ISA on behalf of a child then it is treated as a gift. If the person paying the subscription, the donor, subsequently dies then the gift may be subject to inheritance tax. There are, however, a number of exemptions that would render this unlikely, listed below. These rules apply to gifts generally and not just subscriptions into Junior ISAs.

- **Annual exemption**. Gifts of up to £3,000 per annum are normally exempt. You can also carry forward unused allowances up to one tax year.

- **Gifts out of income**. Gifts paid out of surplus income, where the donor's standard of living has not been reduced as a result of the donation, are normally exempt.

- **Potentially exempt transfers**. If a gift is subject to inheritance tax, the tax payable reduces to zero once seven years have elapsed between the date of the gift and the death of the donor.

Recap

To recap, the maximum you can pay in aggregate into a Cash ISA, Stocks and Shares ISA and an Innovative Finance ISA is £20,000 in the 2021/22 tax year. You can choose any one of these types of ISA, any two or indeed all three if you prefer, as long as the overall ISA allowance isn't breached and as long as you only pay into one of each type in any one tax year.

If you want to pay into a Lifetime ISA or a Help to Buy ISA, there are further restrictions on how much you can pay in to benefit from a government bonus.

Table 3.1 summarises some key points relating to whether you choose a Stocks and Shares ISA, Lifetime ISA or SIPP to save for your retirement. Note that I have not described SIPPs in detail yet, but do so in later chapters in Part Two.

Table 3.1: Funding for retirement – Stocks and Shares ISA v Lifetime ISA v SIPP

	Stocks and Shares ISA	Lifetime ISA	SIPP
Limit on annual contributions/ subscriptions	£20,000	£4,000, included in overall ISA allowance	£40,000 You can carry forward previous three years' unused allowance. High earners and those taking benefits are subject to reduced limits
Tax relief/ bonus on contributions/ subscriptions	None	25%, e.g. contribute £4,000, bonus is £1,000	At highest rate of tax relief, e.g. 20%, 40% or 45% e.g. contribute £4,000, tax relief is £1,000 (20% basic rate tax payer), £2,000 (40%) or £2,250 (45%)
Tax-free growth on investments	Yes	Yes	Yes
Age from when funds can be accessed	No restriction	60 or first time house purchase, or earlier subject to penalty	55 (increasing to 57 from 6 April 2028)

	Stocks and Shares ISA	Lifetime ISA	SIPP
Tax or penalty on benefits/ withdrawals	None	None where the withdrawal is made for permitted reasons, otherwise 25% penalty	25% tax-free and remainder taxed at marginal income tax rate
Included in estate for inheritance tax purposes	Yes	Yes	Usually not

Note that while the Lifetime ISA is marketed with the benefit of a 25% government bonus, a SIPP is marketed as having tax relief at your highest rate of tax. For someone paying basic-rate tax at 20%, a 25% government bonus on a payment into a Lifetime ISA is the same as 20% basic-rate tax relief on a SIPP contribution. If you don't want to worry about the maths, just take at face value that the incentive is the same for basic-rate taxpayers.

Which of the three types of account you choose depends on your personal circumstances. If you are young and don't want to tie up your investments until you are in your late 50s, then you should perhaps focus your savings on a Stocks and Shares ISA, rather than a Lifetime ISA or a SIPP.

If however your sole focus is to save for your first home, with one eye on your retirement, then the Lifetime ISA may well be the most relevant.

Higher earners and the wealthy are still likely to find SIPPs most attractive, not only because of the higher rate tax relief on contributions but also for the inheritance-tax-free status of SIPP funds.

Bed and ISA

Bed and ISA is the name given to a strategy for people with unused ISA allowances, but no spare cash to invest, to use up their ISA allowance by using other investments such as shares in lieu of a cash subscription.

Your investment platform will explain the mechanics to transfer investments from your dealing account to your Stocks and Shares ISA, and may offer reduced dealing commissions to ease the costs of selling and then repurchasing your investments.

As well as dealing commission, other likely costs are the spread, being the difference between the selling and buying price of the shares, and stamp duty of 0.5% on the repurchase.

Don't forget, the sale of personally held investments in this way will be a sale for capital gains tax purposes. This may be useful if, for example, you are trying to use up your annual capital gains tax allowance.

Tax advantages

Capital gains tax

Capital gains tax can be costly for anyone cashing in assets that have risen in value considerably. For investments held personally, for example in a dealing account, capital gains tax of 10% or 20% is chargeable on all capital gains above an annual allowance (£12,300 in 2021/22).

The 20% rate is payable if the gains above the threshold, when added to your income, would take you into the 40% income tax band. Certain assets, such as private company shares, may be subject to a lower capital gains tax. Assets held within ISAs, on the other hand, do not create any capital gains tax liabilities at all.

However, it should be noted that losses on assets held within ISAs cannot be set against capital gains elsewhere in your portfolio.

Income tax

It sounds obvious, but there is no income tax liability on any money you draw out of an ISA.

Transferring your existing ISA

You may find that you are not happy with your existing ISA provider and want to switch to a different one. You may want to bring all your assets into a single place, or want access to lower charges, better service or a wider range of investable assets.

If you are fed up with your current ISA provider, it is relatively easy to change. While there may be costs involved, for example to transfer the investments from one ISA provider to another, quite often you will find that the receiving provider will pick up the transfer costs – up to a certain limit.

Where do I find an ISA provider?

Many DIY investment platforms do not offer Cash ISAs, though one or two do. You will typically find that the best rates for Cash ISAs are available direct from banks and building societies, so you may have to accept that your Cash ISA will sit outside your main investment holdings within your investment platform.

If you take out a Cash ISA, remember to create a diary note for the future to check the market again for the best rates and switch your money to a better account.

Go to one of the comparison websites to compare Cash ISAs. All have comparisons of the top Cash ISAs:

- www.moneysavingexpert.com
- www.moneysupermarket.com
- www.gocompare.com

The websites listed above also have details of which companies offer a Stocks and Shares ISA. A Stocks and Shares ISA is the bread and butter for most investment platforms and the key differentiators are charges and online/mobile functionality, if that is of interest to you. Even a few years after launch, most investment platforms have chosen not to launch a Lifetime ISA, potentially making it simpler for you to carry out your own comparison.

Innovative Finance ISAs are most likely to be offered directly by a P2P or crowdfunding platform but remember my earlier words about exercising caution.

Chapter 19 covers how to choose your investment platform in more detail.

Table 3.2: ISA comparison tool

Name	Date introduced	Subscriptions	Bonus	Age restriction
Cash ISA (adult)	06-Apr-99	Maximum of £20,000 in 21/22. Allowance applies across all types of adult ISA.	None	Must be 16 or over
Stocks & Shares ISA (adult)	06-Apr-99	Maximum of £20,000 in 21/22. Allowance applies across all types of adult ISA.	None	Must be 18 or over
Junior ISA (child)	01-Nov-11	Maximum of £9,000 in 21/22. (However, see transitional rules below the table for savers aged 16 to 18.)	None	Must be under 18
Help To Buy ISA (adult)	01-Dec-15	Maximum of £200 per calendar month, although you can also make an additional initial deposit of £1,000 in month one. Overall subscriptions to the account cannot come to more than £12,000. This counts as part of your overall adult annual ISA allowance.	Bonus of 25% of subscription. Can only be claimed once the value has reached £1,600. Bonus is paid on completion of property purchase (which also means it cannot be used to fund the deposit).	Must be 16 or over

Investments	Withdrawals	Other features / restrictions
Cash	Permitted at any age	You cannot subscribe to more than one Cash ISA in a tax year (but can hold multiple Cash ISAs from different tax years).
Cash, equities, bonds, funds	Permitted at any age	You cannot subscribe to more than one Stocks and Shares ISA in a tax year (but you can hold multiple Stocks and Share ISAs from different tax years).
Cash, equities, bonds, funds	No withdrawals unless child has terminal illness. Converts to an adult ISA at age 18 after which withdrawals are permitted at any age. Child can take control of the Junior ISA from age 16.	It can take the form of a Cash ISA or a Stocks and Shares ISA. A child cannot open a Junior ISA if they already hold a Child Trust Fund (CTF) unless they transfer the CTF into the JISA.
Cash	Permitted at any age. If withdrawal is not used for house purchase, you don't receive the government bonus.	Only open to those who have never owned a property anywhere in the world. For the 25% bonus to apply, the property being purchased must be your first home, be in the UK, be subject to a mortgage and must cost less than £250k (£450k in London*). If the property purchase falls through, the money can be returned to the ISA. You can only hold one Help To Buy ISA at a time. You cannot pay into a Cash ISA and a Help To Buy ISA in the same tax year unless the Cash ISA is closed. You can, however, transfer £1,200 from a Cash ISA to fund the first month's payment. You haven't been able to open a new Help to Buy ISA since 30 Nov 2019, but you can still keep saving into an existing one until 30 November 2029. However, you must claim the bonus by 1 Dec 2030.

Table 3.2: ISA comparison tool, continued

Name	Date introduced	Subscriptions	Bonus	Age restriction
Innovative Finance ISA (adult)	06-Apr-16	Maximum of £20,000 in 21/22. Allowance applies across all types of adult ISA.	None	Must be 18 or over
Lifetime ISA (adult)	06-Apr-17	Maximum of £4,000 per year. This counts as part of your overall adult annual ISA allowance. You cannot pay in after your 50th birthday.	Bonus of 25% of subscription. Bonus paid directly into the Lifetime ISA approximately a month after each payment.	From 18th birthday up to day prior to 40th birthday.

* 'London' in this context means the 33 local authority districts of the Greater London administrative area.

16–18 transitional rules for JISA subscriptions

- In the tax years the child turns 16 and 17, they can subscribe the full JISA limit. From their 16th birthday, they can also subscribe the full adult ISA limit to a Cash ISA.

- In the tax year the child turns 18, they can subscribe the full JISA limit. They can also subscribe the full adult ISA limit to a Cash ISA or, from their 18th birthday, to a Stocks and Shares ISA, a Lifetime ISA or an Innovative Finance ISA.

Investments	Withdrawals	Other features / restrictions
Peer-to-peer loans, crowd funding	Permitted at any age.	You cannot subscribe to more than one Innovative Finance ISA in a tax year (but can hold multiple Innovative Finance ISAs from different tax years).
Cash, equities, bonds, funds	You can make withdrawals penalty-free before 60th birthday for property purchase (or if terminally ill). Otherwise, there is a withdrawal penalty of 25%. No penalty from 60th birthday. If making withdrawal for a property purchase, the withdrawal must be at least 12 months after the first subscription. Property withdrawals must be paid direct to the conveyancer.	If you are making a withdrawal for your first home, it must be in the UK, be subject to a mortgage and it cannot cost more than £450k. You cannot subscribe to more than one Lifetime ISA in a tax year (but you can hold multiple Lifetime ISAs from different tax years). A couple can have a Lifetime ISA each and both use it towards the same house purchase. If the property purchase falls through, the conveyancer must return the withdrawal to the Lifetime ISA.

4

THE DEALING ACCOUNT

The dealing account, sometimes known as a general investment account (GIA) or funds and shares account, is where the DIY investor holds assets that aren't held within a SIPP or ISA. This can be because you have put all you want, or are able, into your SIPP and ISA, or because you are investing in asset classes not allowed in these tax wrappers.

What you can invest in

The world is your oyster when it comes to the range of assets available through dealing accounts. It is only restricted by the investment platform itself. ISAs and SIPPs offer access to literally thousands of funds, investment trusts, government and corporate bonds and quoted shares. Dealing accounts offer all of these and more – including those asset classes that can't be held within the tax-advantaged ISA and many SIPP wrappers, such as shares trading on niche exchanges and derivatives.

The following list summarises what you can invest in with a dealing account.

Dealing accounts – what you can invest in

- Shares issued by companies listed on recognised exchanges around the world
- Unit trusts and open-ended investment companies (OEICs)
- Investment trusts
- Gilts
- Government bonds from countries overseas
- Corporate bonds
- Exchange-traded funds (ETFs)
- Structured products
- Permanent interest-bearing shares (PIBS)
- Real estate investment trusts (REITs)
- Venture capital trusts (VCTs)

How dealing accounts work

Choosing an investment platform

Before setting up an account, you need to decide which investment platform is the best one for your needs. Not all platforms are cheapest for every part of the process, and can be more or less expensive depending on whether you are using them for a SIPP, ISA or dealing account, and depending on the frequency, size and type of investments you are buying or selling.

For most people it makes sense to hold your ISA, SIPP and dealing account with the same investment platform, although DIY investors who are frequent dealers may decide that different providers work out as more cost effective for different parts of their overall investments. Before selecting a dealing account, check the detailed section on comparing investment platforms in Chapter 19 to decide which one is best value for you.

Setting up your account

Once you have decided which provider to go with, registering and applying for an account online should take just a few minutes. You must be over 18 to open a dealing account. You can open the account in joint names with your spouse or partner if you wish, which gives some tax advantages that I will cover in later chapters.

Also, some investment platforms allow you to link accounts so that one person can manage all the family's accounts and also most will have a read-only access facility should you want to give read-only access to your accountant or tax adviser.

Paying money in – cash

Before you can start investing, you need to pay money into your account. You can pay money in, whether online or over the phone, with a debit card, or you can normally send a cheque in the post.

Drip-feeding money into the market on a monthly basis allows you to spread the risk that you buy on a day when the investment you are buying is particularly expensive. You can drip-feed money into the market whether you pay by monthly direct debit or in a lump sum. Where a lump-sum payment is to be drip-fed into the market, the cash sits in the cash account and a monthly instruction to invest is set up.

Paying in shares

You can pay shares into your account by sending the certificates to your investment platform with a stock transfer form, which is available from any investment platform.

This process of moving your shares and funds from one investment platform to another investment platform is called *re-registration*. You can transfer investments held in your dealing account without raising a potential capital gains tax liability and without incurring stamp duty costs, although the investment platform you are leaving may have one-off charges for processing the transfer away from them.

Capital gains tax

This book is not intended to be a tax guide, but I will cover the high-level tax issues you will face as a DIY investor. When you sell an investment for more than you bought it, you create a capital gain. There are, however, a number of exemptions available that mean, in reality, many people escape capital gains tax altogether.

The first and probably most important exemption is your annual capital gains exemption. In the 2021/22 tax year this is £12,300. Everyone gets this allowance, and without stating the obvious (though there is little that is obvious in tax), a husband and wife or two civil partners each get their own allowance in full.

Your taxable gain is the total of your realised capital gains less your annual exempt amount.

The second exemption to be aware of, if you are married or in a civil partnership, is the fact that gifts to a spouse or a civil partner do not create a capital gains liability. The original cost of the investment transfers to the recipient, for calculation of their capital gains tax liability when they ultimately sell it.

You may have already worked out how these two exemptions can be used together to mitigate tax. More on this later.

The rate of capital gains tax payable is 10% if your combined income and taxable gains are less than the upper limit for basic-rate income tax. Any taxable gains above this amount are taxed at 20%. You pay an additional 8% capital gains tax, i.e. at a rate of 18% or 28%, if the gain arises from the sale of residential property other than your primary residence which is free of capital gains tax.

If you own investments jointly with your spouse, any capital gains or losses are shared equally between you.

You can offset capital gains in the current tax year against capital losses in previous years. You must first net off any gains and losses in the current tax year, and only once you have done that can you take advantage of prior-year losses. You can go back up to four tax years, so in the 2021/22 tax year you can offset losses as far back as 2017/18. There are certain restrictions, but the guidance available on HMRC's website is reasonably user-friendly in this area.

There are some tax wrappers and assets that are exempt from capital gains tax:

- Your main home.

- ISA.

- SIPP.

- National Savings Certificates.

- Certain approved share option schemes.

- Betting and lottery wins.

- Private cars, boats, caravans, etc., whose expected life is less than 50 years. (I have never come remotely near to making a gain on any one of these!)

- Tangible moveable property, such as furniture and jewellery, worth less than £6,000.

Typically, where an asset is exempt then any losses in respect of that asset will not be allowed to be offset against a gain.

Note that on your death, no capital gains tax is paid, but inheritance tax is paid on the full value of your assets after using up any inheritance tax-free allowance.

Bed and breakfast

Bed and breakfast is, in the context of investing, the name given to a scheme to crystallise gains or losses on investments to offset crystallised losses or gains elsewhere in your portfolio and reduce your overall liability to capital gains tax.

This term originates from a practice, common years ago, when investors would sell investments to crystallise a gain equivalent to the capital gains tax allowance, go to bed, wake up, have their breakfast and then buy exactly the same investments back again. The going to bed, waking up and having breakfast bits were, of course, all superfluous. The idea was to take advantage of the annual capital gains tax allowance without being out of the market for any period of time.

HMRC moved to stop this loophole in 1998 by introducing a rule that says if you buy back the same investment within 30 days, then the sale is disregarded for capital gains tax purposes.

Bed and spouse

Bed and spouse is not quite as saucy as it sounds, but still represents solid tax planning. Married couples and civil partners can minimise their capital gains tax bill by making the most of any unused tax allowances the other party may have. This can involve giving investments to the spouse or civil partner with unused tax allowances, made easy by the fact that transfers between spouses and civil partners do not crystallise a capital gains tax liability. There are no time restrictions involved, and you can transfer investments to a spouse or partner who can then sell them immediately to take advantage of this.

There is no liability to stamp duty on the transfer, nor does this create a potential inheritance tax liability. The original base cost of the shares will carry over to the recipient, so the ultimate gain or loss is not affected. All you are doing is making best use of two capital gains tax allowances instead of one. Using any or all of the unused allowances of a spouse or civil partner to reduce your own tax bill is known as a *bed and spouse* strategy.

Gifts between spouses and civil partners can also cut the couple's overall income tax bill. Putting income-generating investments into the name of the spouse or civil partner with the lowest total income will mean tax on that investment income will be paid at a lower rate.

Example: Bed and spouse – sharing allowances

Katie and Peter are married. Katie has a large portfolio of shares and wants to sell shares in a pharmaceutical company that have increased from £20,000 to £40,000.

If she simply sells the shares herself she will crystallise a capital gain of £20,000, £7,700 of which is liable to capital gains tax after her £12,300 capital gains allowance is taken into account. As she is a higher-rate taxpayer she will pay capital gains tax at 20%, totalling £1,540.

By transferring half of the shares into Peter's name she pays no capital gains tax at all, as her capital gain is now just £10,000. Peter also has a £10,000 capital gain that is within his annual allowance.

Peter is earning less than Katie and only pays basic-rate tax. So, if the capital gain on the sale of the shares had been greater and exceeded both their annual allowances, it would have been more tax efficient for the majority of the shares to be held in Peter's name, as he would have been liable to capital gains tax at only 10% and not the 20% payable by Katie.

5

THE SIPP –
SELF-INVESTED PERSONAL PENSION

SIPPs have become the retirement savings product of choice for investors wanting pensions that offer transparency, control, choice and competitive pricing.

A SIPP, which stands for self-invested personal pension, is a type of personal pension plan. SIPPs differ from personal pensions offered by insurance companies by virtue of the fact that they put you, the DIY investor, in complete control of where you invest your retirement savings.

SIPPs warrant more discussion than ISAs and dealing accounts, so the next three chapters each look at different aspects of SIPPs. These are:

- Chapter 5: SIPP overview and tax relief benefits

- Chapter 6: Transferring pensions into and out of a SIPP

- Chapter 7: Taking benefits from a SIPP

SIPP overview

SIPPs offer exactly the same tax advantages as traditional personal pensions, meaning basic-rate, higher-rate and additional-rate taxpayers can get 20%, 40% and 45% tax relief on contributions respectively. There are some nuanced differences for those paying Scottish income tax, but the principles are broadly the same.

Investments held within a SIPP also grow free of income and capital gains tax.

While mainstream pension plans typically only offer access to a predetermined selection of funds, SIPPs allow you to invest in a far wider range of assets, including unit trusts, OEICs, shares, bonds, exchange-traded funds and commodities. Online SIPPs allow you to view and adjust your holdings 24 hours a day, giving real-time pricing of the assets held in your SIPP portfolio.

A quarter of the value of a SIPP can be taken as a tax-free lump sum from the age of 55 (increasing to age 57 from 6 April 2028). SIPPs also give you the flexibility to remain invested in stocks, shares and other investments while you draw a pension income, as an alternative to buying an annuity. All in all, this means SIPPs are an extremely efficient way of saving for the long term.

You can have a SIPP even if you are a member of a company pension scheme – for example, if you want to save more than the amount offered by your employer's pension scheme. However, if you are a member of a company pension scheme it normally makes sense to take advantage of that offer before setting up any alternative top-up arrangements.

You can use a SIPP to buy commercial property, whether it be your business premises or purely as a stand-alone investment, although to do this you will need what is often called a *full* or *full-fat* SIPP. You will find that most DIY investment platforms offer a low-cost online SIPP, but few if any of these will allow investment directly in commercial property. Costs for full SIPPs are normally considerably higher than their online counterparts due to the more complex administration involved.

Key reasons to have a SIPP

- Tax relief on contributions at your marginal rate of tax

- Investments grow free of income and capital gains tax

- A quarter of the value of your SIPP fund can be taken tax-free from the age of 55 (age 57 from 6 April 2028)

- Pension income can be drawn directly from your SIPP instead of buying an annuity

- Benefits payable on death are typically free from inheritance tax (though beneficiaries will have to pay income tax where the deceased was 75 or older when they died)

- Investment flexibility, before and after retirement

- Transparency of charges

- Low cost

- You are in control

- All your pensions are accumulated in one place

More esoteric investments, such as unlisted company shares and some unregulated collective investments, can also be held within a SIPP. Again, a full SIPP may be required if these assets are to form part of your SIPP portfolio. Access to these investments has become more challenging in recent years, even in the full SIPP market, as a result of rulings made by the Financial Ombudsman Service and in the courts. These place due diligence requirements on SIPP operators before they're able to allow customers to purchase individual esoteric investments. They potentially make the SIPP operator liable for compensation if the due diligence was insufficient. As a result, most operators have become more restrictive in terms of the investments they allow.

If you want to minimise charges, I would challenge anyone to find a lower-cost pension than a low-cost online SIPP invested in a handful of mainstream tracker funds. Charges can be significantly lower than the much-lauded stakeholder pension with its 100 basis points (1%) annual management charge.

Other pension products charge even more than stakeholder pensions, and if you are unfortunate enough to have an old-style pension that is invested in what are called *initial* or *capital* units then you could be paying as much as 3% or 4% per annum in charges.

Key reasons not to have a SIPP

- You are in a company pension scheme that meets your pension needs

- You can only access your benefits from the age of 55 (age 57 from 6 April 2028)

- You can only access your SIPP in the form of a lump sum and taxable income

- SIPPs can't invest in certain assets, such as residential property

What SIPPs can invest in

SIPPs offer access to a wide range of investments from around the world, such as:

- Shares quoted on HMRC-recognised stock exchanges

- Unit trusts and OEICs, also known as collective investments

- Government bonds/gilts

- Corporate bonds

- Permanent interest-bearing shares (PIBS)

- Warrants

- Investment trusts

- Exchange-traded funds
- Exchange-traded commodities

Full SIPPs may also be able to hold:

- Commercial property
- Unlisted shares
- Unregulated collective investments

The current list of what SIPPs can invest in was fixed in 2006. But in the years running up to these new rules, the government had consulted on whether it should radically open up what SIPPs could invest in.

At the time, the press printed story after story suggesting that holiday homes both in the UK and abroad, racehorses, works of art, fine wine, luxury yachts, flats for your kids and many more eye-catching investments might all be allowable in SIPPs, enabling you to acquire these investments with the assistance of tax relief.

Each week the stories became more outlandish, but the government seemed intent on maintaining their position that virtually anything would be acceptable when it came to investing in SIPPs.

This period of intensive press coverage just served to raise the profile of SIPPs in the eyes of pension savers and their advisers. People weren't interested in traditional personal pensions or stakeholder pensions anymore, with their usually limited range of investment options. Everyone wanted a SIPP.

I was quite vocal at the time – both in the press and in discussions with HMRC – that I thought this move was madness. I was taking phone calls from Spanish property agents asking if we would run a branded SIPP for them. Considering the significant property slump in Spain following the banking crisis of 2007/08, I imagine the story wouldn't have ended well.

Anyway, good sense did eventually prevail and I am led to believe that two events in the run-up to the 2005 Pre-Budget Report, now called the Autumn Statement, caused ministers to change their mind. I was involved in both of those events.

The first involved a *Sunday Times* article, or, more specifically, its headline. One of the big Scottish insurance companies had put out a press release saying that approximately £10bn of pension money would be invested in residential property come the day when the new rules were introduced.

The journalist who wrote the story asked me to check her article for technical facts. The article was fine, but I did have a problem with the headline. It read 'Residential property in SIPPs to cost Treasury £4 billion'. The simple logic applied by the headline writer was that tax relief at 40% would be granted on this £10bn, so that was the cost to the Treasury. The point I made was that most of the money that would be used to buy residential property was already in SIPPs up and down the country and hence tax relief had already been granted. My point was ignored but apparently this headline acted as a wake-up call for ministers about the scale of what they were about to sanction.

While I can probably claim the moral high ground on the dodgy headline saga, I struggle to do so with the second part of this story. I received a call just before the 2005 October half-term from a BBC researcher asking if I would be interviewed on *Newsnight* to discuss the impending pension rule changes. Their plan was to do a feature on racehorses, boats, Spanish holiday homes and vintage cars being held in SIPPs. The thought of being on the wrong end of a Paxman-style grilling didn't appeal, but I did see an opportunity to put forward the voice of reason.

After checking my diary, I realised I was in Spain on holiday that half-term week, so it was all academic. "No problem," the researcher said, "we will meet you in Puerto Banus when we are doing the boat piece and interview you then." So I agreed and duly met up with Justin Rowlatt, the BBC presenter, one Thursday morning in Puerto Banus where we boarded a luxury 65-foot Princess Yacht that the BBC had chartered for the day and set out to sea.

I was asked to stand on the boat, holding a glass of champagne and the filming began. You can probably see what is coming and, to be honest, as the first sip – no pun intended – went down, so could I.

When the interview was aired, the edit did not include my protestations for a government U-turn and instead were replaced with some general musings about pension simplification being welcome. What was evident to BBC viewers, however, was that the chief executive of this particular SIPP provider would be quids in if these changes went ahead. Look at him celebrate on what could well be his own boat, sipping champagne, soon to be an asset of his SIPP no doubt.

Apparently, ministers were apoplectic with rage and, very soon, I started to hear rumblings that a U-turn was on the cards. On 5 December 2005, the U-turn was announced, so at least the end result was the right one.

This U-turn introduced the concept of taxable property. It was not the outright ban I had hoped for, but instead, tax charges would be imposed should a SIPP invest in any assets that HMRC deemed inappropriate. Residential property clearly fell on the wrong side of the line, as did racehorses, vintage cars and most other esoteric assets at the heart of the press excitement. But the rules around some other investments, such as unquoted shares, were – and still are – horrendous and unworkable.

Unlisted shares

It is possible to hold unlisted shares in a SIPP, but there are complex rules surrounding when it is permitted to do so. Many SIPP providers do not allow unquoted shares because of the complexities of ensuring these rules have not been breached.

Tax position of SIPP investments

The tax rules on investments within a SIPP are the same as for a Stocks and Shares ISA. In summary:

- Interest on cash is received gross, with no deduction of tax.

- The investments held within a SIPP are able to accumulate tax-free. It is the eventual benefits that are paid out from the SIPP that are subject to tax.

- Interest on bonds/loan stock can be received gross by the SIPP as well as cash. If tax is deducted in error the SIPP provider can reclaim the tax deducted.

- No capital gains tax is paid on the disposal of an investment in a SIPP (including shares and property).

- No tax is deducted from dividend income in a SIPP and there is no additional tax liability outside the SIPP in relation to dividend income received within it.

- If you have a SIPP that allows investment property, rental income from this can also be received by the SIPP without any income tax liability.

- The tax position on income and gains made on overseas investments will vary depending on the status of the SIPP holder and the country in which the investment is held. However, a variety of tax concessions can be available to UK pensions in respect of overseas investments.

Tax relief and contributions into SIPPs

One of the key incentives offered by the government for pension saving is the tax relief provided on the amounts paid into pensions by savers and their employers.

When you or your employer make a payment to a pension this is known as making or paying a *contribution*. You will recall from Chapter 3 that paying into an ISA is often called a subscription, but the principle is the same.

You don't have to pay contributions to use a SIPP – you can instead just transfer funds from pensions held elsewhere. However, if you want to increase the value of your pension, as well as aiming to maximise the growth you achieve from your investments, topping up your pension with contributions will help.

Contributions can be paid to a SIPP as a one-off payment called a single contribution, or an instruction can be set up so that an agreed amount is paid each month, referred to as a regular contribution. Most SIPPs have modest minimum amounts for both single and regular contributions.

To make a contribution to a pension and claim tax relief, basic eligibility requirements must be met, but most UK residents will be eligible. There are limits on the amounts that can be paid into a pension and receive tax relief each tax year.

The concept of an annual allowance was introduced in 2006 and this is now the main control mechanism used by HMRC to ensure that you don't pay too much into your pension. If your total personal and employer contributions exceed the annual allowance then you may face a tax charge on the excess, although you may be able to carry forward any unused annual allowance from earlier tax years.

The standard annual allowance is £40,000 in the 2021/22 tax year, however you now need to be aware of a couple of additional wrinkles recently introduced by the government.

The first of these is linked to the *pension freedoms*, introduced at the start of the 2015/16 tax year – more on this later. Broadly speaking, anyone who has taken advantage of these freedoms will see the amount they can pay into money purchase schemes like SIPPs reduced from £40,000. The contribution limit fell to £10,000 for the first two years of the pension freedoms and then to £4,000 from the 2017/18 tax year. This shouldn't be a major issue for most, as few people draw money out of their SIPP at the same time as contributing. However, anyone considering withdrawing a large chunk of their pension while in their late 50s needs to bear in mind the restriction it will place on their ability to rebuild their pension.

In the 2016/17 tax year the government introduced a horribly complex set of rules designed to limit the contributions of those with an income exceeding around £150,000. From 6 April 2020 the £150,000 threshold was increased to £200,000. Explaining these rules, known as the *tapered annual allowance*, is beyond the scope of a book focused on DIY investing. Suffice to say that if you've had a combined income (and this doesn't just mean your earnings, but also income from investments and other sources) in the last few years approaching six figures you should check with a tax adviser (or the HMRC website if you are feeling brave) whether you are affected, as your annual contribution allowance may reduce from £40,000 to as little as £10,000.

As well as the various annual allowances, there is a further restriction on how much you can pay into a SIPP, or indeed any other type of pension: personal contributions, though not employer contributions, are restricted to a maximum of 100% of your *relevant earnings*, or £3,600 – whichever is higher. Relevant earnings in this instance excludes investment or pension income.

Contributions – personal contributions

Personal contributions made to a SIPP are paid net of basic-rate income tax (20% for the 2021/22 tax year).

For example, if you pay a personal contribution of £800, then your SIPP provider will reclaim £200 from HMRC and credit this amount to your SIPP cash account once it has been received.

You will be treated as having made a contribution of £1,000 to your SIPP for tax purposes. This is the total of the net personal contribution and the basic-rate tax reclaim associated with it.

This reclaim of basic-rate tax will typically be credited to your SIPP between six and 11 weeks from the date you pay the contribution. This delay reflects the timing of the monthly tax reclaim process carried out by your SIPP provider.

Any higher-rate relief that you are entitled to is usually reclaimed via your self-assessment tax return.

In the above example, if you are a higher-rate taxpayer you will claim back an extra £200 via your tax return, making the cost of a £1,000 contribution equal to £600, as you would expect if you are paying a 40% rate of tax. If you are an additional-rate taxpayer you will reclaim £250 via your tax return, making the cost £550 for a 45% taxpayer.

You should be aware that there is no relief for either employer's or employee's National Insurance if a personal contribution is paid.

Most SIPP providers won't accept any personal contributions to a SIPP once someone has reached their 75th birthday, since they are not eligible for tax relief from that age.

Contributions – employer contributions

Your employer may also pay contributions into your SIPP.

All employer contributions are payable gross. By gross, I mean that if your employer agrees to pay you a £1,000 SIPP contribution, then that is how much they actually pay. As we have seen above, if you want to pay £1,000 as a personal contribution you only pay £800 and the tax system then kicks in to ensure you get the correct level of tax relief.

The employer will normally receive tax relief on any contributions they pay to your SIPP as a normal business expense and you, the employee, will not normally be taxed on these contributions.

Employer contributions are not restricted by the 100% of UK earnings limit (or the £3,600 maximum), but they do count towards the annual allowance usage.

If an employer contribution is made on your behalf, no PAYE tax or employer's or employee's National Insurance is paid. So you may hear people say that an employer contribution is more National Insurance efficient than a personal contribution, which it is.

Contributions – annual allowance

The annual allowance is used by HMRC as a means of restricting tax relief on pension contributions. The annual allowance is £40,000 for the 2021/22 tax year.

As touched on above, your annual allowance may be less than £40,000 if you are a very high earner or if you have already made use of the pension freedoms. In some cases your annual allowance could be as low as £4,000 so it is worth checking with a tax adviser if you think this could be relevant to you.

You will need to ensure that your total pension contributions are within your annual allowance in the relevant tax year, with the additional test that your personal contributions do not exceed the higher of 100% of your relevant earnings, or £3,600 in that tax year.

Contributions – carry forward of unused annual allowance

In some circumstances it is possible to reduce the impact of the annual allowance through the use of carry forward.

Carry forward allows unused annual allowance from each of the three previous tax years to be swept up. The exact amount will depend on your annual allowance in that tax year and the amount you've already paid into your pension in relation to that period.

As long as you were a member of a UK pension scheme (whether or not you were contributing to it) in the tax year from which you wish to carry forward unused annual allowance, and you have sufficient UK earnings in the tax year in which you make the contribution, then you can use carry forward if your contributions exceed the annual allowance in that tax year.

Carry forward cannot be used unless you have exceeded the annual allowance in the current tax year.

HMRC has a useful calculator which allows you to calculate how much unused allowance you have. Just search 'HMRC unused annual allowance' and you will find it on HMRC's website.

If the annual allowance in any tax year is exceeded (after any available carry forward has been used up) then an annual allowance tax charge will apply. The mechanics for paying this tax charge are beyond the scope of this book, but they will be driven by your tax return and the net result will be to cancel out any tax relief on excessive contributions.

Contributions – salary sacrifice

A salary sacrifice arrangement can be a tax-efficient way in which to pay contributions to a SIPP, and its origins lie in the differing treatment of National Insurance between employer and personal contributions.

This option is only available for those who are an employee of a business and not for a partner or a sole trader.

A salary sacrifice arrangement involves an individual agreeing to give up some salary or bonus in exchange for their employer making a contribution to their SIPP.

This results in the individual being in receipt of lower taxable earnings, and so benefiting in two ways:

1. They will pay less in National Insurance contributions.

2. Compared with making an equivalent personal contribution to their SIPP, the payment of an equivalent employer contribution allows the individual to invest the full contribution amount immediately. A corresponding personal contribution would have been paid net of basic-rate tax relief and there would have been a delay in the tax element being paid by HMRC to the SIPP.

The employer will make a saving in the amount of employer's National Insurance contributions it pays. This can mean it is possible to negotiate with the employer to see whether it is prepared to pass on some or all of its saving in employer National Insurance contributions by way of an additional employer contribution to the SIPP.

Salary sacrifice involves a change to an individual's contract of employment, so will need to be documented. If the arrangements are not established properly and in the right circumstances, they could be challenged by HMRC.

Higher earners should take care when using salary sacrifice as it is possible that the contributions may be treated as earnings for the purposes of the tapered annual allowance calculation.

6

TRANSFERRING EXISTING PENSIONS INTO, OR OUT OF, A SIPP

This is the moment, I am afraid, where you need to take a deep breath and dig out all of those old dusty files marked 'Pensions', if you have any. Hopefully you may be pleasantly surprised at how much has accumulated in your various pensions over the years – or maybe not.

Transferring your various pensions into a SIPP can make sense for a number of reasons. The average person in the UK will have 11 employers through their working life, which means most people end up with lots of pension pots, none of which on their own is of any great value.

The paperwork that pensions can generate knows no bounds, so consolidating your plans into one place will help you to keep track of your retirement savings and give your postman a break.

Being able to see all of your investments in one place makes it easier to plan for your retirement. It also makes it easier to build a portfolio of investments that accurately reflect your retirement objectives and appetite for risk.

You may want to transfer your existing pensions into a SIPP if they are invested in a pension with high annual management charges, or with limited investment options.

There are, however, several reasons not to transfer your existing pension benefits into a SIPP.

Unfortunately, there is unlikely to be a simple answer to the question of whether you should transfer or not. Search the internet and you will find plenty of conflicting messages on the issue of transfers, some of which are accurate, but many of which are born out of a lack of understanding or an irrational fear that all transfers are bad.

Pension transfers – the rules

The transfer of benefits into or out of a SIPP is permitted as long as the benefits come from or go to another suitable pension arrangement.

Benefits can be transferred between any registered pension schemes. A registered pension scheme is one that agrees to follow UK pension legislation when registering with HMRC. A transfer involves the transferring scheme paying a transfer value to the receiving scheme.

To effect a transfer of an existing pension into your SIPP, you need to tell your SIPP provider the name, address and reference number of the pension to be transferred.

Most transfers are made in the form of a cash transfer between the two schemes. But it is possible to transfer assets to avoid having to sell them in order to transfer – a process known as an *in-specie* transfer. This is normally only possible where both the transferring and receiving schemes are SIPPs.

While a cash transfer may take two to three weeks, an in-specie transfer is a more complicated process and can take several more weeks. The benefits of an in-specie transfer are similar to those of an ISA and dealing account re-registration, which we covered in earlier chapters.

Types of pension scheme

Your first job is to find out what type of pension you have. The next job, which is rather more challenging, is to find out what the transfer value is and what benefits you will be giving up by transferring it to a SIPP.

The key types of pension scheme you will come across are as follows.

Company pension schemes

- **Occupational pension scheme.** This is a pension scheme established by an employer. It typically takes one of two forms, either a **money purchase scheme**, sometimes referred to as a defined contribution scheme, or a **final salary scheme**, sometimes referred to as a defined benefit scheme. An occupational pension scheme is typically established as a trust and has a board of trustees who look after the members' interests.

- **Money purchase scheme.** This would typically see both you and your employer contributing a percentage of your salary into the scheme. There are no guarantees as to the level of benefits you will receive at retirement. You accumulate a pot of money and, at retirement, see what that can provide in the form of a tax-free lump sum and a pension.

- **Final salary scheme.** This would typically see you build up benefits for each year of service based on your final salary. This may be something like 1/80th of your final salary for each year of service. So, if you work for 40 years, you will get a pension of half of your final salary. There are variations on this theme where benefits may be based on the average of your salary near the end, or throughout the whole, of your career. If you're looking to transfer a final salary pension scheme, if it has a transfer value of more than £30,000 you will need to take regulated financial advice before being able to move the funds. You'll find out more about exactly what a *transfer value* is in coming pages.

Final salary transfers

The FCA, which regulates financial advisers, has had final salary transfers in its cross hairs for some time now. Concerned by some examples of demonstrably bad advice, the FCA expects advisers to start from a position that a transfer out of a final salary scheme is not suitable. Many advisers no longer offer this advice due to the increased regulatory scrutiny and professional indemnity insurance costs.

I am not a fan of this overly paternal approach. There are many valid reasons why it could be in someone's best interest to transfer from a final salary scheme into a SIPP. The individual may be in poor health, have other assets such that the guarantee nature of the pension is not needed, be single or as in many cases, may want to pass the value of the pension down to the next generation. Also, not enough consideration is given to how healthy the funding of the final salary scheme is nor how prosperous the sponsoring employer is. Failure of the latter will almost certainly cause major problems to the former.

An adviser's report substantiating a transfer from a final salary scheme is now so complex that you can't see the woods for the trees. A major part of this report sets about trying to assess the value for money of the transfer value in rather an illogical way. What the regulator has never really accepted, nor given any credence to, is that every final salary scheme has a scheme actuary at its helm. One of the professional responsibilities of the scheme actuary is to certify that the basis on which transfer values are paid represents fair value for money, making general assumptions about the age, sex, marital status and mortality of scheme members. To my mind, the emphasis and focus of the advice should be about how important the guarantees are to the individual, how they may differ from the typical member (e.g. if they are single then they won't benefit from the spouse's pension, whereas they would get credit for this in the transfer value), how well funded the scheme is, the appetite for risk when investing the transfer value and the perceived value of creating an inheritable asset.

Personal pension schemes

- Alternatively, your work-based pension scheme may be a **group personal pension scheme** or a **group stakeholder scheme**. Technically speaking, these pensions are simply groups of individual personal pension schemes (see below) that happen to be under the umbrella of the employer. These are also money purchase schemes, but the key difference is that, unlike occupational money purchase schemes, they do not have boards of trustees and are regulated by the Financial Conduct Authority (FCA), rather than, or in some cases as well as, the Pensions Regulator.

- **Personal pension scheme.** This is a pension scheme that is established by an individual with a pension provider. Contributions can be paid by the pension saver and their employer and there are typically no guarantees as to the benefits that will be available at retirement. Stakeholder pensions and SIPPs are both personal pensions.

- **Other.** Other schemes you may see reference to in your bundle of papers include Section 32 plans, executive pension plans, retirement annuities, AVCs (additional voluntary contributions), FSAVCs (free-standing additional voluntary contributions) and appropriate personal pensions. For all intents and purposes, these can be treated as personal pensions.

Issues to consider before transferring your existing pension benefits into a SIPP

- **Charges.** Compare the charges under your old pension with the SIPP you are considering. This comparison is not always easy, but you should have a go. In most cases the cheaper option becomes apparent very quickly.

- **Transfer penalty.** Does your old pension have an exit or transfer penalty for leaving? There is now a cap of 1% on most exit charges for the over 55s.

- **With-profits investments.** If your pension fund is invested in a with-profits fund and you are near to retirement age then there may be merit in staying invested in the plan until the end of the term. It is notoriously difficult to assess the merits, or otherwise, of a with-profits fund and, to do this properly, specialist financial advice is probably the only way forward.

- **Guaranteed annuity rates.** Annuities are now far less popular as a source of retirement income than they were five years ago. The pension freedoms have played a part in this, but so have the low levels of income provided by most annuities. If your existing pension offers a guaranteed level of income, the second of these considerations falls away, and will potentially be much more valuable than the flexibility offered by the pension freedoms rules. Does your plan entitle you to any attractive guaranteed annuity rates that would be lost on transfer?

- **Defined benefits.** Are you in a defined benefit scheme? If so, the decision whether or not to transfer is a lot more complicated and you'll probably be required to take financial advice.

- **Options at retirement.** Does your existing pension give you access to income drawdown, or must you buy an annuity in order to get a pension?

- **Protected tax-free lump sum or low retirement age.** Does your existing pension allow you to take more than 25% of your pension fund as a tax-free lump sum or to take benefits before the age of 55? If so, this will normally be lost if you transfer.

- **Cash or in-specie transfer.** If you decide to transfer, will it be a transfer of cash or will you transfer assets (in-specie transfer) as well as cash?

- **Your health.** If you transfer your pension while you're terminally ill, HMRC may decide that your pension becomes liable for inheritance tax.

Charges and transfer penalties

What drove me out of working for an insurance company was spending my days designing long-term savings and pension products with charging structures and exit penalties that should have meant nobody in their right mind would buy them. It didn't matter that these products were awful because they were sold by an in-house sales team who were well skilled in selling the sizzle of what were rotten sausages.

I am pleased to say that the sort of products I am describing here have now been outlawed, so any new policies you might take out will not have these problems. But there are many old-style pension policies out there that still carry these toxic features. When a pension policy was sold, it generated a big lump of commission to the salesperson. As well as the commission it paid, the insurance company also had expenses to cover in setting up the policy, such as IT, administration and marketing costs.

It didn't take a marketing genius to work out that selling a pension policy where the first few years' premiums are eaten up in charges would be as easy as selling Jürgen Klopp t-shirts outside Goodison Park.

To cover this massive cost of getting pension business on their books, insurance companies used a variety of very innovative solutions that masked the real impact of the product's charges. These charging structures enabled the insurance companies to recoup their expenses and earn a handsome profit over the lifetime of the policy. The real challenge came when the policy was transferred mid-term to another pension arrangement, as many were. A transfer penalty was needed to ensure that the insurance company was not out of pocket. This transfer penalty is best described as the difference between what is called the *fund value* and the *transfer value*.

The fund value is the headline figure you get on annual statements. It is the *Parkers'* car guide showroom value of the car on your drive. It is what the car is worth unless you actually want to sell it, when you need to look at the trade-in price.

Similarly, the real value of your pension policy is the transfer value, as this is what the insurance company will pay if you want to transfer to another pension arrangement.

What are the key messages here? First, only ever believe the transfer value. Any other valuation provided is an illusory one.

Second, the transfer penalty is just a discounted value of charges that you would have paid in any event. That is, you will suffer these charges whether you stay or whether you go. Your only choice is whether you pay these charges on the drip over the lifetime of the pension policy, or as a lump sum when you transfer your pension benefits to another pension scheme.

So, while it may sound a controversial statement, not transferring your pension benefits because you will suffer a transfer penalty is often flawed logic.

As we have seen above, the government has introduced a 1% cap on most exit charges from pension policies for the over 55s.

With-profits investments

With-profits policies were sold as low-risk funds, run by insurance companies, invested in a combination of shares, property, bonds and cash.

The deal between the with-profits policyholder and the insurance company goes something like this – the policyholder pays a premium that is invested in a broad spread of investments. Dependent upon the returns that these investments achieve, annual bonuses are declared each year by the insurance company. Terminal bonuses for those reaching the end date of the policy are also declared.

The idea is that with-profit funds provide a smoothed investment return. Some of the investment return in the good years is held back to increase the investment return in the bad years. Some of the investment return is also held back to pay the terminal bonus on maturity or retirement, which is really a loyalty bonus for staying the term of the policy. In the case of a with-profits pension, this could be 30 or 40 years.

If you choose to transfer a with-profits pension to a SIPP, or indeed any other pension scheme, then the insurance company is likely to impose what is called a *market value adjustment*. Even though they pay you those annual bonuses year after year, they aren't actually for keeps. Well they are, but only if you continue as a premium-paying policyholder for the full term of the policy. If you don't fulfil this obligation then, at the insurance company's discretion, they can and almost certainly will claw back some of the bonuses they have previously awarded. They may also make an adjustment to take account of investment conditions, again under the banner of a *market value adjustment*.

While the return over recent years of most with-profits policies has been very poor, if you are very close to retirement there may be merit in sticking with the policy to get your full entitlement of annual and terminal bonuses. The further away you are from the retirement date set on the pension policy, the harder it is to justify sticking with what can be best described as an investment from a bygone age.

Guaranteed annuity rates

Some pension policies, particularly old policies such as retirement annuities, contain valuable guaranteed annuity rates. These guaranteed annuity rates were inserted into policies when interest rates were a lot higher than they are today. They weren't intended to be particularly valuable, but they have proven to be.

If you have a pension policy with a guaranteed annuity rate, unless you are in poor health or are totally against buying an annuity, then it is probably worth keeping that particular pension policy where it is.

Options at retirement

Most personal pensions, and all self-respecting SIPPs, offer access to the pension freedoms, which give you a huge amount of flexibility over how you withdraw money. They allow you to take a tax-free lump sum and keep the residual monies invested, while drawing an income from your pension pot, which is known as income drawdown.

More later on these options, but if you decide that you are likely to opt for them in favour of buying an annuity then this may tip the balance in favour of you transferring your existing pension benefits into a SIPP.

Transfers – pensions in payment

It is possible to transfer a personal pension scheme, which of course includes a SIPP, even if benefits have commenced using income drawdown.

You should also note that you can't transfer benefits from a defined benefit scheme once you have started receiving your pension income.

Once you have bought an annuity the option to transfer to a SIPP is lost.

Transitional protection and transfers

Transitional protection is the name given to certain exemptions and protections from the pension limits and allowances introduced in April 2006. Some of these may be lost on transfer. Transitional protection is covered in greater detail in Chapter 7.

Transfers – in-specie transfers

Although most transfers are made in the form of a cash payment between the pension schemes, it is possible for the schemes to agree to an in-specie transfer of assets, in lieu of cash, as part of the overall transfer.

This may be useful where there is a desire to change your SIPP provider but not the underlying investments.

An in-specie transfer allows the existing investments, such as a portfolio of stocks and shares or a commercial property, to be transferred from one SIPP to another without the need to realise them for cash, avoiding the risk of potentially being temporarily out of the investment markets at an inopportune time.

Not all investments can be transferred in specie since they may not be assignable or capable of being re-registered into the name of the new SIPP. Some investments, such as unquoted shares, may not be acceptable to the new SIPP provider. This makes it important to check that your new SIPP provider will accept all the investments in your existing SIPP.

The in-specie transfer is also likely to take a significantly longer time to complete than a cash transfer between schemes. This can have practical implications on matters such as the payment of drawdown pension income, since the new scheme will not be able to commence income payments until the transfer of assets has been fully completed and documented.

Transfers – overseas schemes

Transfers from a UK-registered pension scheme can be made into a qualifying recognised overseas pension scheme (QROPS). Transferring to a QROPS may make sense if you are emigrating to another country, but there are situations where it makes more sense to keep your money in the UK, so it is worth taking advice before doing so.

In many cases you have to pay a tax charge of 25% to the UK government just to make the transfer. You should also beware of any companies claiming to be able to liberate your pension or invest in high-returning funds through a QROPS. These schemes will generally have enormous hidden fees, some are in breach of HMRC's regulations and a number are ways of defrauding you out of your pension.

7

TAKING BENEFITS FROM A SIPP

Overview

Unless you are incapacitated or in serious ill health, you cannot normally commence benefits from a SIPP until you have reached the age of 55. The earliest age at which you can take benefits will increase to 57 from 6 April 2028.

When commencing benefits, you can normally take part of your benefits tax-free. The remaining balance must normally be taken as a taxable income.

For many years, the income you could take from your SIPP was subject to restrictions with the aim that it would be payable for the rest of your life. However, the introduction of the *pension freedoms* in April 2015 radically altered the position. Now, pension savers have the option of taking as much, or as little, as they wish out of their pension at any time.

If you have a SIPP, you can choose the way in which your income is provided in various ways:

- A tax-free lump sum and taxable flexi-access drawdown income.

- A tax-free lump sum and taxable capped drawdown pension income – although this is only available in limited circumstances.

- A tax-free lump sum and a taxable annuity from an insurance company.

- An uncrystallised funds pension lump sum, part tax-free and part taxable.

Reference to a payment being taxable means it will be subject to PAYE income tax, which will be deducted at source by your SIPP provider.

Normal minimum pension age

The normal minimum pension age is 55. SIPP benefits can be taken from this age, or any time afterwards, irrespective of whether you are still working. This minimum age will increase to 57 from 6 April 2028.

Lower retirement ages for specialist occupations are allowed, for individuals who retain a protected pension age from the old pension regime – for example if they were a professional sportsperson in a pension scheme prior to the current pension rules being introduced in April 2006. Where a protected pension age is held then it is possible to commence benefits before the age of 55.

The right to a protected pension age can be lost if the benefits are transferred out to another pension scheme without meeting a number of requirements, so care is needed.

Lifetime allowance

There is no absolute limit to the benefits that may be provided under a SIPP, or indeed any registered pension scheme. But if the total value of all benefits, under all registered pension schemes, exceeds the lifetime allowance then there will be an additional tax charge, called the *lifetime allowance charge*, payable on the excess.

The lifetime allowance for the 2021/22 tax year is £1,073,100.

Where you exceed the lifetime allowance, if you leave the excess in your SIPP to be drawn as a taxable pension, the lifetime allowance charge is 25% of the excess. You will then pay income tax in addition on any amounts you take from your SIPP in the future.

You can, however, choose to draw the excess as a lump sum, which would be subject to a lifetime allowance charge at 55% of the excess, with no further tax to pay. Your SIPP provider will deduct the lifetime allowance tax charge before the benefits are paid.

A simple example may help you understand how the lifetime allowance works. It relies on the concept of benefit crystallisation events. These normally occur when benefits start to be taken from a particular pension scheme.

Example

Fred has £150,000 in a personal pension and starts taking pension benefits in 2021/22. He takes this in the form of a £37,500 tax-free lump sum and £112,500 goes into income drawdown. As the lifetime allowance is £1,073,100, this benefit crystallisation event uses up 13.97% of Fred's lifetime allowance.

If Fred has other pensions, then these will be tested against the lifetime allowance when they are crystallised. Once he has used up 100% of the £1,073,100 lifetime allowance from benefits, the lifetime allowance charge kicks in.

Tax-free lump sum

Once the decision has been made to take benefits, it is possible to choose a number of options.

The two main ways in which you can access your pension are through income drawdown from the SIPP and by using the funds in your SIPP to purchase an annuity from an insurance company.

Whichever of these options is chosen, it is usually also possible to receive a tax-free lump sum (properly known as a pension commencement lump sum) from your SIPP.

For most people, the tax-free lump sum is quite simply 25% of the value of the SIPP, but more technically it is the lower of:

- 25% of the value of the fund used to provide the benefits, and

- 25% of your unused lifetime allowance.

Higher lump-sum benefits may be available if you have a protected tax-free lump sum – these higher lump sums emanate from some company pension schemes prior to 2006 that were protected as the pension rules were simplified.

A tax-free lump sum cannot be taken with the intention of using some, or all, of it to fund a large increase in pension contributions. This is called *recycling* and may result in significant tax charges.

Income drawdown

After taking a tax-free lump sum from your SIPP, and assuming you don't buy an annuity, the funds remaining in the SIPP will be used to provide income drawdown benefits.

Income drawdown can be used in many ways, but the most common model involves using your pension to generate a regular retirement income by reinvesting your money in income-paying funds. The income you receive will depend on the fund's performance and is not guaranteed for life.

There are two main types of income drawdown product: flexi-access drawdown or capped drawdown.

Capped drawdown is only available if you started in drawdown before 6 April 2015 and so, for those just now starting to take benefits or those doing so in the future, this is no longer an option.

In both flexi-access drawdown and capped drawdown, the part of the SIPP fund you don't withdraw remains invested in your SIPP tax-free.

Flexi-access drawdown

Flexi-access drawdown allows you to take as much or as little out of your SIPP at any time you choose. So, if you really think it is a good idea, you could choose to withdraw all of the funds from your pension in one go.

When considering how much to withdraw you need to think about some important factors:

- Whatever you withdraw is subject to income tax – if you take out a lot you could end up paying 40% or even 45% tax (or even higher if you live in Scotland).

- Once you have taken funds out of your SIPP they lose valuable tax advantages. The funds will no longer be sheltered from inheritance tax and any investments you make in your own name may be subject to capital gains tax and income tax.

- Funds in your SIPP are better protected in the event of bankruptcy, and taking cash out of your pension may have an impact on means-tested benefits to which you would otherwise have been entitled.

- As soon as you take any flexi-access drawdown pension payments out of your pension, the amount you can pay each tax year into a money purchase pension, like a SIPP, falls significantly from £40,000. The reduced limit was £10,000 for the first two years of the pension freedoms but has been further restricted to £4,000 from the 2017/18 tax year.

Capped drawdown

If you're still in capped drawdown then your maximum annual pension is calculated based on 150% of what a notional annuity would pay, the precise amount being set by the Government Actuary's Department (GAD).

These notional annuity rates take into account the yield on government stock, namely 15-year gilts, and the SIPP member's age. But they do not reflect the enhanced annuity terms that might be available from an insurance company in the open market, which may take into account other factors such as the SIPP member's postcode, state of health, smoking and drinking habits.

The capped drawdown limit is set at the date on which pension benefits are first taken, and applies for each 12-month period ending on the anniversary of that date. This period is sometimes referred to as the drawdown year.

While you're in capped drawdown the amount you can pay into SIPPs and other money purchase pensions each tax year stays at £40,000. If you go over your annual capped drawdown limit you'll automatically convert those funds into flexi-access drawdown. This may not be of any concern to you, but if you were planning to pay significant amounts into your SIPP in the future you should consider that you'll be restricted to a much lower maximum each year following conversion to flexi-access drawdown.

Other considerations

Drawdown pensions of both types can be paid monthly, quarterly, annually or as ad hoc single payments.

Unlike a lifetime annuity, the drawdown pension level is not guaranteed. The amount you're withdrawing should be reviewed regularly – in the case of capped drawdown your scheme administrator is required to review the maximum amount you can withdraw at regular intervals.

Your SIPP can be used to purchase a lifetime annuity at any point, even after drawdown has been commenced.

Partial drawdown

Partial drawdown allows investors who do not need all their tax-free cash or income straightaway to take benefits from only part of their pension pot.

Example

Assume Sally, age 60, has £200,000 in her SIPP. She needs £25,000 for a new car, but doesn't need to draw any income from her SIPP as she is still working. She elects to crystallise 50% of her SIPP, this being £100,000. This provides her with a £25,000 tax-free lump sum and she elects to take no income from her flexi-access drawdown fund, which is worth £75,000. After she has taken her tax-free cash, 57% of her total SIPP – £100,000 out of £175,000 – remains uncrystallised.

Uncrystallised funds pension lump sum (UFPLS)

The introduction of a new option for taking benefits, the horribly named UFPLS, was touted as one of the most significant changes introduced by the pension freedoms in April 2015. While it is heavily used by savers in schemes that don't offer drawdown, I remain unconvinced of its value elsewhere.

Simply put, an UFPLS is a single lump sum from your SIPP made up of a tax-free element of 25% of the amount paid from the pension, with the other 75% being subject to income tax.

Example

If we return to Sally from the example above, instead of choosing the partial drawdown option, she might instead choose to take an UFPLS for the £25,000 she needs to buy her car. The exact amount she'd need to withdraw would depend on her tax code and allowances, but we'll assume that a £28,000 UFPLS would do the job.

We know this would provide her with a tax-free element of £7,000 (25% of £28,000) and a taxable element of £21,000 (75% of £28,000). If we assume that £3,000 in tax is deducted from the taxable element then she ends up with £7,000 (tax free) and £18,000 (after tax), so £25,000 in total.

When compared to the partial drawdown option, the UFPLS works better by using up less of Sally's tax-free allowance – she's only used up £7,000 of her 25% tax-free allowance, rather than £25,000. However, in order to get hold of her £25,000 she has had to withdraw £28,000 from her SIPP because of the taxable element.

Which option is best for you will depend on whether it is more important to you to keep as much in the SIPP as you can – so partial drawdown may be best – or whether you want to retain as much of your tax-free lump sum as you can for future use – in which case you may prefer UFPLS.

Taking an UFPLS will restrict the amount you can pay into your SIPP to £4,000 per year in the future, as you have flexibly accessed your pension. If instead you took the whole amount as a tax-free lump sum under partial drawdown, your ability to contribute wouldn't be affected.

For those in a pension already offering drawdown, which would include all SIPPs, the UFPLS isn't really that significant an introduction. Pretty much the same can be achieved by taking a tax-free lump sum payment from some of your pension and withdrawing all of the funds that had been moved into drawdown in one go. One thing to be aware of is that, if you choose this option, you're likely to receive the tax-free and taxable payments a few days apart. With the UFPLS you'll receive a single payment.

Lifetime annuities

All or part of your SIPP can be used to purchase a lifetime annuity from an insurance company. This can be done either at the point benefits commence from the SIPP, or after a period during which a drawdown pension has been taken.

Purchasing a lifetime annuity involves passing your pension fund to an insurance company that, in return agrees to provide you, the annuitant, with a pension income for the rest of your life. You can choose to have a pension income for your spouse, partner or other beneficiary after your death.

Each insurance company decides what level of pension they are willing to provide, depending upon a number of factors. These include the individual's age, personal circumstances, the amount used to purchase the annuity and the type of annuity selected. The annuity terms offered by insurance companies can vary considerably, so it is important to shop around to obtain the best deal.

There are many options you can choose from when purchasing an annuity. These will include:

- **Level or escalating pension income.** Choosing an escalating annuity means that your income can increase each year to help protect against inflation. But because the income will increase in the future, the starting level of an escalating annuity will be lower than that of a level annuity. This difference can be substantial. When considering this, it is important to balance the advantage of rising future long-term income against the disadvantage of a lower initial income level. This decision may be influenced by factors such as your health and life expectancy, any views on the long-term effects of inflation and an understanding of the fact that you will be more active in the early years of your retirement so are likely to want to be spending more money.

- **Type of escalating annuity.** The income can be increased by a fixed annual rate, such as 3% per annum, or in line with some measure of inflation such as the Retail Prices Index (RPI) or limited price indexation, which provides inflation protection capped at an upper limit, again possibly 3% per annum.

- **Investment-linked income.** Some annuities offer the potential for income to increase if the underlying investments perform well. This is balanced against the risk that the annuity income may fall if the investments do not perform well.

- **Single life or joint life.** A proportion of an annuity can be paid after death to a surviving spouse/partner or possibly another beneficiary. This is called a joint life annuity. The level of the survivor's pension is usually expressed as a percentage of the annuitant's income, typically half or two-thirds. The income under a single life annuity ends on the annuitant's death. The income under a joint life annuity will continue for longer if the spouse/partner/beneficiary outlives the annuitant, and as a result the initial level of annuity income will be lower than for a single life annuity.

- **Guarantee periods.** Provision of a guarantee period means that, if the annuitant dies during the period of the guarantee, the income due for the remainder of the guarantee period will still be paid. In some circumstances this can be paid as a lump sum; if not, the income will be paid as a continuing pension.

- **Enhanced annuity**. Depending upon your personal circumstances, it may be possible to receive an increased annuity. A number of factors will affect whether this is available. The most common are the health of the annuitant and their family and their lifestyle history. This could be one of the few rewards for a lifetime of drinking, smoking and unhealthy eating!

- **Payment frequency and timing**. An annuity can be payable monthly, quarterly, half-yearly or annually in advance or in arrears. If the annual in-advance option is chosen, a lower income will be paid than if the annuity income is being paid monthly in arrears.

- One final choice worth mentioning is the **flexible annuity**, which is one of the less well-known choices introduced by the pension freedoms. It differs from a lifetime annuity by offering the option for the income received to fall in value rather than staying level or increasing. The option of a falling income might not seem particularly attractive but it might work well for someone who wishes to take an income from one of their pensions before other sources of income kick in, for example the state pension or a final salary scheme. The annuitant might choose to take a higher initial level of income on the basis that this would fall once the other sources of income were available.

I've seen very little evidence that this option has been popular, either with insurance companies or annuitants, hence it is not attracting much attention.

If a flexible annuity does appeal, one thing to bear in mind is that buying one will reduce the amount you can pay into money purchase pensions in the same way as flexi-access drawdown or UFPLS. Your contribution limit is unaffected if you take a lifetime annuity.

Advice and Pension Wise

If you're still finding yourself confused over the choices for accessing your pension that are available to you, you have a couple of options for further assistance. One is to seek advice from an FCA-authorised financial adviser. If choosing an adviser isn't for you, another option is a government-backed guidance service called Pension Wise. Using online materials, phone-based support and face-to-face appointments, it aims to guide those approaching retirement in understanding how to make decisions which are right for them. As the focus is on helping those close to retirement, appointments are only available for those aged 50 and over. However, the broader online material can be read by all.

More information can be found here www.pensionwise.gov.uk/en or by phoning Pension Wise on 0800 138 3944.

Tax on pensions

When taking a pension income from your SIPP, the payments will be paid subject to income tax. This applies regardless of whether the benefits are being paid as flexi-access drawdown, capped drawdown or an annuity.

Where drawdown pension payments are being paid, your SIPP provider will be responsible for the income tax deductions from the pension income. The insurance company providing the annuity will deduct this tax from annuity payments.

An emergency tax coding will normally be applied until your SIPP provider or annuity provider has been provided with a tax coding by HMRC. Any under- or overpayment of income tax can be dealt with either via your self-assessment tax return or by completing a form that allows a claim to be made in the same tax year you were paid.

Depending on your circumstances, you'll need to complete either a P50Z, P53Z or P55 to reclaim your tax.

Your SIPP provider or annuity provider will issue a form P60 after the end of each tax year to help with completion of your self-assessment tax return.

Individuals who are resident abroad may live in a country that has agreed tax concessions with HMRC. This may allow your pension to be paid gross, with tax only being deducted in the relevant country of residence.

In order to benefit from any double taxation agreement with another country, you will need to negotiate a special tax coding with HMRC and may wish to take relevant advice to establish what is applicable for your chosen country of residence.

Which option to choose – flexi-access drawdown or lifetime annuity?

The first question you should ask yourself before taking benefits is, "Should I take any at all?"

Once you start drawing benefits, you will get a tax-free lump sum and can also take a pension income. If you spend this money, great. But if you just put it in the bank or in your dealing account, then this money may be subject to income tax, capital gains tax and, in the event of your death, will form part of your estate for inheritance tax purposes.

That said, most people aren't fortunate enough that they can afford to live without touching their pension once they have stopped working. So let us assume you have decided to start drawing benefits and now need to decide which option to choose – lifetime annuity or flexible drawdown.

For this section we'll ignore the UFPLS, as a similar outcome can be achieved through flexi-access drawdown and only a limited number of customers choose it. Most people are faced with a choice of flexi-access drawdown or lifetime annuity.

The choice for most boils down to whether you want certainty of income for the rest of your life, or whether you want an income that could be higher but might also need to drop if you take out too much under flexi-access drawdown.

The price of the certainty of income throughout your life offered by a lifetime annuity is that you forgo the capital, which stays with the insurance company when you die. The quid pro quo of the volatility of flexi-access drawdown is that you retain control of the capital to invest how you choose and to pass on to your heirs after your death. And with the changes to death benefits that were introduced with the pension freedoms, which to my mind were so generous they may not be sustainable, the ability to pass on to heirs will be a powerful draw towards drawdown for many.

When you buy an annuity, you need to decide at the outset whether or not to include a beneficiary's pension. Should your beneficiary die before you do, then paying more for the beneficiary's benefit will have been wasted.

If you die while in flexi-access drawdown, the full fund can be left to your spouse, heirs and other beneficiaries you have nominated. Subject to lifetime allowance limits, the value of your SIPP can normally be passed on tax-free on your death, although if you die after you have hit 75 the recipients of the pension or lump sum will have to pay income tax on the proceeds.

The income you can receive from an annuity has declined in the last decade or so, and these days you get less bang for your buck. People are living longer and the impact of this is magnified by the current low-interest environment.

Income drawdown has grown in popularity in recent years as annuity rates have steadily declined, forced down by increases in longevity, lower interest rates and stricter rules governing how much capital insurance companies offering them have to hold. The introduction of flexi-access drawdown and changes to the taxation of death benefits have also been hugely influential in driving the popularity of drawdown over annuities.

Pros of drawdown

- You can remain invested in the stock market for longer, not tied to gilt returns for what could be a retirement of three decades or more. Equity investment has the potential to give protection against inflation.

- You are able to pass on your pension fund as an income or lump sum after death. There is usually no tax to pay if you die before 75, but this is subject to income tax thereafter.

- You can avoid cashing in the entire fund when annuity rates seem poor or while you don't qualify for an ill health enhanced annuity rate.

- It is possible to withdraw as much or as little as you choose, enabling you to remain invested for longer and to manage income flow to minimise income tax.

Cons of drawdown

- There is no guarantee that income will be sustained.

- The value of your SIPP will be subject to fluctuations due to market movements.

- You may still end up buying an annuity later on, and annuity rates could be even worse by then.

The decision between drawdown and a lifetime annuity boils down to a clear choice. If you want certainty, buy an annuity. If you are willing to accept the fact that your income may increase or decrease and that you will be exposed to the vagaries of the stock market, then drawdown is more likely to be suitable for you.

I make no apologies for the fact that I am pro drawdown. People save for their retirement in all sorts of ways, many of which are discussed in this book, and not all involving a pension. If someone suggested that you convert your ISA, which you have been using to save for your retirement, into an annuity when you retire, you would think they had gone mad. So there is no reason why people should be forced to buy an annuity when they have saved in a pension account, such as a SIPP.

I campaigned for the scrapping of compulsory annuity purchase for over 20 years and I am delighted we have finally reached a point where people can choose the option that suits them best.

People would never dream of converting personal savings and investments into an annuity, but it is quite normal to convert a personal pension pot that hitherto has had no guarantees into a guaranteed income for life. Now that there is no legislative requirement to buy an annuity, my starting point is that there needs to be a compelling case to do so.

Incapacity/serious ill health

Benefits can be taken from a SIPP before the age of 55 on the grounds of incapacity or serious ill health, subject to satisfactory medical evidence.

Incapacity

To be eligible to take pension benefits on the grounds of incapacity, evidence must be provided that you are unable, and will continue to be unable, to carry on your occupation because of physical or mental impairment.

You will then be entitled to a tax-free lump sum from your SIPP and can use the balance to provide a retirement income in the same way as someone over 55 can.

Serious ill health

To be eligible to draw benefits on the grounds of serious ill health, evidence must be provided that you are expected to live for less than one year.

If this is the case, you are entitled to the full value of your SIPP as a tax-free lump sum, to the extent that you have sufficient unused lifetime allowance. For funds over the lifetime allowance, a tax charge of 55% will be deducted before the balance is paid out as a lump sum.

Incapacity or serious ill-health benefits are not available from any part of your SIPP in drawdown.

Protection from the lifetime allowance

When the new, *simplified* pension rules introduced the concept of the lifetime allowance back in April 2006, some people already had pensions that exceeded the new £1.5m lifetime allowance by a considerable way, or had pensions that were likely to exceed this limit by the time they came to take lump sum and pension benefits.

To ensure that pension savers did not suffer any retrospective loss, a number of transitional protection measures were introduced. There was as much legislation, if not more, created to deal with protecting the lifetime allowances of those who had already built up big pension pots as there was to establish the new system itself.

Two forms of transitional protection against the new lifetime allowance were introduced – *enhanced protection* and *primary protection*.

The good news is that most people affected by this would have an adviser, so this is not normally an issue for DIY investors. And the time period to register for such protection expired on 5 April 2009, so if you haven't got this protection, there is nothing you can do about it.

The lifetime allowance is under constant political scrutiny and has been reduced by various governments from £1.8m at its peak to a low of £1m in 2016/17 and 2017/18. The allowance has since been linked to inflation, so it has risen a little to £1,073,100 in 2021/22, still some way below its peak. In the most recent Budget, the Chancellor removed the inflation link, thereby freezing the allowance until at least 2026.

That is the bad news. The good news is that it is well established that if the lifetime allowance is reduced again, some form of protection will be available for existing pension savers who have large SIPP funds. Indeed, further forms of protection were introduced at the same time as previous lifetime allowance decreases in 2012, 2014 and in 2016.

PART THREE

THE DIY INVESTOR'S TOOLKIT – THE INVESTMENTS

8

FUNDS

The last few chapters have looked at tax wrappers and dealing accounts – or products you can use as a DIY investor. In the case of the tax wrappers, these may help you to save money on tax and charges, but they will never make you money. It is the underlying investments into which you put your money that generate those spine-tingling financial wins and losses.

Different types of investment have different degrees of sophistication and complication. If you are new to DIY investing then you can achieve all of your investment goals without looking any further than funds, whatever your risk appetite.

If you want access to the stock market, but want to leave the selection of individual company shares to the experts, then funds could well be for you. By pooling your money into a fund with many thousands of other investors you can get access to highly skilled fund managers, while still staying in control of the sectors you invest in and the managers you use.

Competition between fund managers to deliver the best performance is fierce. The more successful the fund, the more money the manager makes, which means their interests and yours are very much aligned. If you do not see yourself having the time, energy or inclination to trade individual company shares, investing through funds can be an efficient way to get exposure to all sorts of markets across the globe – including equities, bonds, commercial property and many other asset classes.

Or you may wish to invest some of your money through funds and some directly into equities and other investment types. Whichever way you want to construct your portfolio, getting exposure to the fund that is right for you has never been easier. These days, most investment platforms offer access to several thousand funds across a bewildering array of sectors, geographical regions, asset classes and investment strategies.

Even sophisticated DIY investors will often use funds in their portfolio, if only to access sectors or geographical regions that can be very difficult to gain exposure to by investing directly in equities. If you want exposure to a fast-growing emerging market, for example, then a fund is one of the best ways to do this.

You may not even want to use funds that pay fund managers high fees to manage your investments. Many successful DIY investors ignore star fund managers and opt for the increasingly fashionable passive or tracker funds that have ultra-low charges and mimic the return that a particular sector of the market is delivering (see Chapter 9). Either way, investment platforms offer more funds than you will ever need.

Almost all of the funds available through investment platforms can be held in your SIPP, ISA or dealing account.

Background

The first pooled investment funds were created in Holland in the 18th or 19th century, depending on which historian you believe. Similar funds soon emerged elsewhere in Europe, with the concept taking root in the USA in the 1890s.

The UK's first pooled investment funds were investment trusts, such as the Foreign & Colonial Investment Trust, which was founded in 1868 and is still going today under the new name of F&C Investment Trust. These first investment trusts were, and still are, closed-ended funds, which means that the number of shares in the investment trust is the same from one day to the next. We will cover investment trusts in Chapter 10 and see that this closed-end structure plays a significant role in how the price of an investment trust moves.

The first open-ended funds emerged in the USA in the 1920s. They were different from their closed-ended counterparts because they allowed new shares, or units, to be allocated to investors when they invested in the fund.

Traditionally, the main funds available to UK investors have been unit trusts and open-ended investment companies (OEICs). You may also see these referred to as ICVCs, which stands for Investment Company with Variable Capital.

The main attraction of an open-ended fund is that its price is not driven by supply and demand. For instance, you may have seen big increases in the price of a share that is tipped in a national newspaper. That is because the share price is driven by supply and demand. A fund can receive a similar commendation in the same national newspaper and its share price shouldn't move – it is the value of the underlying investments that the fund holds that dictates the share price of the fund.

Different types of fund

As mentioned earlier, the most common types of open-ended funds available in the UK are unit trusts and OEICs. Neither unit trusts nor OEICs are listed on the stock exchange; their price is instead reflected in the value of the underlying investments that they hold. The price is normally set once a day, this being called the valuation point.

There are structural differences between unit trusts and OEICs. When you put money into a unit trust you receive units, whereas in OEICs you receive shares. Investors in unit trusts are called unit-holders, while investors in OEICs are called shareholders.

Another key difference is the fact that unit trusts have a buy-or-offer price and a sell-or-bid price. OEICs have a single price.

For all intents and purposes, there is no difference between an OEIC and a unit trust to the DIY investor, and the former is now the preferred structure in the UK for funds. For the rest of this chapter, we will focus on OEICs and you can assume that the terms 'fund' and 'OEIC' are interchangeable, unless stated otherwise.

Different share classes

A fund can have sub-funds with different share classes, to reflect different charging structures, currencies or distribution. They often have different share classes for institutional and retail investors, with charges higher for the latter.

Funds typically offer two main ways for shareholders to receive returns – the income class and the accumulation class. You can normally tell by looking at the product name: it should say 'INC' for income, or 'ACC' for accumulation.

Income

The income class of a fund pays, or distributes, dividends or interest depending upon the type of fund. These payments are made directly into a cash account with your investment platform. Payments are made shortly after the fund's distribution date. If you don't hold the fund through an investment platform, the income will be paid direct to your bank account.

Income class shares could be particularly useful if you are at a stage in your life where you need income from your investments, rather than growth.

Accumulation

The accumulation class rolls your dividends or other income back into your fund, rather than pay it out to you.

Accumulation class shares are the ones to go for if your sole aim is to grow your portfolio. By opting for accumulation units or shares, your money gets reinvested in the fund by the fund manager, without dealing costs, initial charges or bid/offer spreads.

The mechanics of buying, holding and selling funds

Buying shares in a fund is easier than buying a flight on a discount airline. Once you have done your research and decided on the fund you want to buy, simply log into your investment platform, choose the account or tax wrapper you want to buy the fund through, identify the fund and then click on the buy button. It's that easy.

Settlement

Buying and selling funds is not as instantaneous as buying and selling equities, due to the fact that funds are normally only priced daily. For example, if you invest in a fund at 10.30 am on a Tuesday, you will buy shares in the fund at the forward price, determined at the fund's valuation point, which is normally midday.

At some time after the valuation point, often overnight, the fund manager will confirm the price with your investment platform, and therefore the number of units or shares you have purchased. If you invest after the cut-off point for a given day's valuation point, your order will be rolled forward to the following day's valuation point.

Switching funds

Why is the settlement process relevant? Well, you will hear talk of fund switches, where investors sell one fund and buy another. This process is not quite as slick as you may hope. When you sell a fund, you will normally need to wait at least until the following morning for your account to be credited with cash in order to go on and invest the proceeds in another fund or investment.

Before that point in time, your investment platform simply won't know how much money you are going to receive from the sale. In reality this means you will be out of the market for a day, and possibly even two days, when you switch funds, while you wait for the sale proceeds to reach your account and then the buy transaction to go through. It's not normally a major issue, unless you are very unlucky, and you may also be lucky and have valuations move in your favour.

This settlement period is only really relevant if you want to take your cash away from your investment platform immediately after selling the fund or funds. In these circumstances, your investment platform will wait until it has received the hard cash from the fund manager before it hands it over to you.

Research and fund selection

When you buy a fund, you are paying a fund manager to do the stock selections precisely because you do not want to do it yourself. So when it comes to funds, the only research you have to do is around what fund to invest in. As with equity investments, it pays to spread your fund investments across several funds so you can even out the risk in your portfolio.

To decide what funds to go for you will first need to decide your investment objectives and the sort of portfolio you need to deliver these objectives within your risk appetite. Your portfolio might easily include funds covering UK, global and emerging market equities, corporate bonds and commercial property. These investment classes are considered in greater detail in later chapters.

Once you have worked out the type of asset allocation you think you will need, you will then have to find the right funds to meet these objectives. This will involve looking for funds, or individual fund managers, with a good track record in the areas of the market you are looking to invest in.

There are a number of places you can go to find fund recommendations. Some investment platforms will suggest their own lists of funds. These are often presented as model portfolios, or recommended funds lists to meet different objectives and risk profiles.

Best-buy lists are particularly useful for investors who aren't paying for financial advice. They help bridge the gap between advice and effectively throwing darts at a dartboard to pick investments. Guidance from best-buy lists gives these people a tool by which to make more considered investment decisions.

More thought goes into compiling these lists than you might think. They tend to involve experts researching the market and comparing costs, fund manager track record, the size of the team supporting the fund manager and the investment process.

There are no guarantees that these best-buy lists will make you rich but they can help you narrow down the investment universe when considering where to put your money. Anything that gives a helping hand to the retail investor has to be applauded.

Another approach is to look at independent research from organisations such as Morningstar, Trustnet and Citywire, all of which have historic data, factsheets and other information on fund managers' performance. Specialist investment magazines and websites such as *Shares, Investors Chronicle* and *MoneyWeek* also have articles containing research and analysis of fund managers.

You can also easily see which sectors everyone else is investing in. The Investment Association (IA) provides a lot of market data on its website, www.theinvestmentassociation.org, showing the most popular sectors.

Most weeks, the financial pages of the broadsheets cover which funds to buy and sometimes which to sell.

You also need to understand what the fund is aiming to do and what it is allowed to invest in. Every fund has a set of investment objectives that the manager is required to follow. This is explained on the fund's factsheet, which you can find easily by searching the internet for the name of the fund and the word 'factsheet'. These factsheets are also available from your investment platform.

The factsheet will show how well the fund has performed against other funds in its sector over various time periods up to and including five years. It will also show the portfolio breakdown, dividends, fund size, top holdings and charges.

The cult of the star fund manager

No one is top of the tree forever, but some managers seem to have a knack for performing better than the pack through good times and bad. Whether this is down to skill or luck is a matter of debate in the investment industry. Some investors do not believe that there is any statistical likelihood of a particular fund manager outperforming the market over a long period. Others argue the very best, most experienced managers will deliver the goods more often than not.

The archetypal star fund manager is Anthony Bolton, former manager of the Fidelity Special Situations fund. For 28 years Bolton was a money-making machine. Someone who invested £1,000 in his fund at launch in 1979 would have been sitting on £148,200 by the time he quit the fund in 2007. Bolton's record is a fabulous one, but he is one of thousands of managers, most of whom have come nowhere near achieving his returns.

The hard fact about fund management is that a substantial proportion of fund managers underperform the index or benchmark they are trying to beat.

Even Bolton managed to blot his copybook when he returned to the fray at the helm of the Fidelity China Special Situations fund in 2010, being forced to apologise to investors for below-benchmark returns at the end of 2011 when he admitted his bets on the Chinese economy decoupling from the West had been wrong. More recently, Neil Woodford has had a similar fall from grace, caused by an over exposure to unlisted shares.

Another problem with star fund managers is they can become victims of their own success as more investors' money piles in. Some experts argue that the larger a fund becomes, the harder it is for the fund manager to add any real value. They become powerless to make significant market-beating returns because the fund is simply too big and unwieldy.

Citywire allocates a star rating to fund managers, rather than to the funds that they manage. This probably says it all. Like Premier League footballers, my view is that the great ones are handsomely paid and worth every penny. The rest make up the numbers.

Supporters of the concept of the star fund manager point to the big names that have delivered market-beating returns more or less consistently over a long period. And putting your faith in people who can demonstrate some level of success over a number of years surely feels more logical than giving your money to a fund manager whom you have picked at random.

I like to keep an eye on what shares these star fund managers hold in their funds, if only to generate ideas for my own portfolio. If you do look at the top holdings of the larger funds, it should probably come as no surprise how many common investments they all share. This points to one of the risks of investing in actively managed funds – which is that if many fund managers are simply doing the same thing, holding the same shares, then you may be buying a fund that just tracks a particular investment market, e.g. the UK equity market. If so, there are far cheaper ways of doing this by investing in a much cheaper passive or tracker fund.

Neil Woodford is one of the best-known fund managers in the UK and someone who built up a reputation for principle-based investing. If you looked at his fund's holdings in the run-up to the bursting of the dot-com bubble when he was running funds at Invesco Perpetual, you would not find any technology stocks. Similarly, in the run-up to the banking crash, he had no holdings in banks. With hindsight some call this genius, while others call it principled investing. But the truth is, in the run-up to both of these events, his significant underperformance against his peers led to many investors voting with their feet and no doubt ruing that decision.

Woodford is an important person to consider when talking about investing as he ran into trouble in 2019, causing thousands of investors to have their money locked away for over six months.

His Equity Income fund was hugely popular as retail investors hoped he would repeat his success at Invesco Perpetual by running funds under his own company. Unfortunately, performance started to tail off as Woodford deviated from his proven investment process of picking larger companies, adding smaller and illiquid holdings to the portfolio, as well as picking some stocks that experienced problems.

As more investors started to ask for their money back, Woodford sold many of the larger holdings to raise cash to pay back investors, meaning the portfolio became even more dominated by the remaining illiquid holdings. He couldn't keep pace with the redemption orders and the fund was suspended and subsequently wound down, leaving Woodford's reputation seemingly irreparably damaged.

There are important lessons to be learned from this event. Always check to see if a fund manager is sticking to their stated investment process and not deviating in style, so keep checking the factsheet to monitor the underlying portfolio holdings. Don't put all your money with one manager and don't assume that someone who has been successful in the past will always continue to do so in the future.

Passive or active fund management

In the past, as a DIY investor you have had two clear choices – either choose your own equities, or leave a fund manager to invest your money on your behalf. This was quite a stark choice, with no real middle ground.

But a relatively recent alternative to a fund manager actively managing investments on your behalf has emerged, where funds are invested without active management – a process called passive fund management. Funds managed in this passive fashion are called *index trackers* and are covered in more detail in Chapter 9.

These passive funds are now proving to be a real alternative to the active fund-management industry and pose a serious challenge to it. Best of all, the costs of passive funds are a fraction of active funds – not least because there are no star fund managers to pay.

So, before trying to figure out which is the best fund or who is the best fund manager, there is a question to ask yourself first – do you even want to pay the fees that come with active fund management?

While some passive funds do operate under the structure of an OEIC, the majority are structured in a different way, as *exchange-traded funds*. That is why I have split passive or tracker funds off from this chapter and cover them in detail in Chapter 9.

Sectors

With thousands of funds available to DIY investors, it is important to know your way around the different sectors, regions, themes and strategies they are based upon.

Sectors are a way of arranging funds into groups that are invested using similar strategies or objectives.

The Investment Association (IA) sectors divide funds into more than 30 (including Unclassified) different sector groups. These sectors can be divided into broader groupings, as shown in Figure 8.1. The IA website will give you precise definitions of the aims of the funds within each sector and the parameters they are required to operate within. These parameters may be limits or minimum levels of certain types of assets, the size of the stocks held, i.e. small or large cap, or geographical restrictions on the investments they hold.

Let's now look at the four broad groupings from Figure 8.1 in more detail.

Growth

Growth funds can be equity or mixed asset in make-up. Growth funds cover sectors such as UK All Companies, UK Smaller Companies, and various overseas equity funds based on geographical region or on themes such as Global Emerging Markets. Mixed asset funds have set percentages that can be invested in different asset classes, typically equities and fixed income investments such as corporate and government bonds and cash.

UK All Companies funds, for example, are defined by the IA as "funds which invest at least 80% of their assets in UK equities which have a primary objective of achieving capital growth".

However, funds within any IA sector may have widely varying asset mixes, strategies and risk profiles.

Income – fixed income/equity/mixed asset

Income funds invest in fixed-income assets such as corporate and government bonds, in dividend-generating equities or a combination of the two. Fixed-income sectors include UK Gilts, Sterling Corporate Bonds and Sterling Strategic Bond funds.

Funds in the Sterling High Yield sector are riskier, with at least 80% of their assets required to be in UK corporate bonds rated below, or more risky than, BBB–. Funds in the Global Bond sector are, as their name suggests, made up of overseas corporate bonds.

Funds in the UK Equity Income and Global Equity Income sectors must aim to achieve a yield of income in excess of 100% of the yield of the FTSE All-Share and MSCI World Index respectively on a three-year rolling basis and 90% on an annual basis.

Companies issue corporate bonds as a cheap way to raise finance, attracting investors with returns that are higher than cash on deposit. The coupon, or interest, is the amount paid each year by the company until the end of the bond's term, when the original capital is also repaid. If you hold corporate bonds until they expire you will know exactly what you will get out of them – the annual coupon for the number of years left on the bond plus the return of the amount that the company originally borrowed, provided the company does not go bust along the way.

But corporate bond funds buy and sell bonds before they expire, and their values change depending on how likely the market thinks it is that the company backing the bond is likely to go bust and default. The value of corporate bonds is also impacted by interest rates in the wider economy. Lower interest rates from banks means demand for high-yielding corporate bonds goes up and vice versa, meaning the value of the bond itself can also go down and up – an increase in interest rates normally means a fall in the value of a corporate bond fund, and vice versa.

Government bonds work in exactly the same way – UK government bonds are called gilts – with the market risk being that the country defaults on its debts. Government, or sovereign, debt in developed countries has historically been a relatively low-return, unexciting part of the economy. Returns are lower because of the lower perceived risk in a whole country not having the money to pay back what it owes.

Corporate bonds are generally perceived as being less risky than equities, and investing in corporate bonds through a corporate bond fund reduces your overall risk.

Figure 8.1: Fund sectors

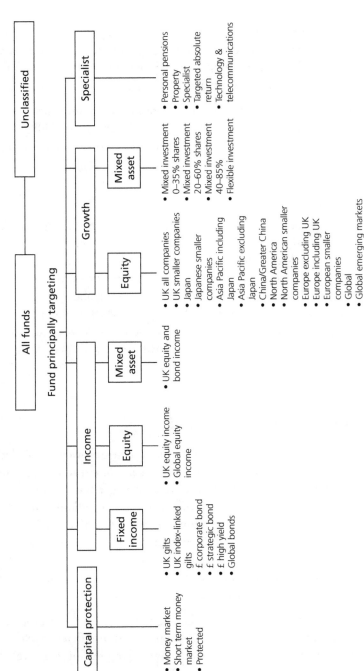

Source: Investment Association

Capital protection

Funds in the capital protection grouping of IA sectors include money market or cash funds and funds offering capital protection by locking in gains, or guaranteeing capital and linking returns to an index.

Some people refer to money market funds as cash funds, which is not strictly correct. Money market funds invest in cash, bonds with only a short term to maturity and other so-called debt instruments. There is some capital risk to these funds.

Specialist

The IA's specialist sector grouping covers a range of sectors that do not fall into any of the others. Funds investing in specialist sectors, such as Technology & Telecommunications, and Property, fall into this category. So do funds defined by a particular investment process such as Absolute Return funds, which aim to achieve an above-zero return at all points in the investment cycle. Targeted Absolute Return funds are supposed to smooth out returns by using derivatives and short-selling strategies, although many have delivered dismal performances in recent years.

Commercial property funds

Commercial property is a sensible component of a well-diversified investment portfolio, and the easiest way to get exposure to it is through a commercial property fund. The fund manager buys commercial properties with leases on shops, offices and other buildings and the rent it receives is paid out to investors as income. As with other income-generating funds, income can be withdrawn or reinvested into extra units or shares in the fund. Accumulation versions of a fund take dividends or other forms of income and rolls them up back into the fund, thereby increasing its price.

One advantage of having at least some exposure to commercial property is the fact that the sector theoretically performs in different cycles to other parts of the economy, thereby diversifying risk in your overall portfolio. Commercial property funds are generally considered less risky than equity funds.

That said, commercial property funds performed terribly along with virtually every other class through the credit crunch, proving the theorists wrong when they fell around 40% in around 15 months between 2007 and 2008.

Commercial property funds also hit the headlines in the aftermath of the EU referendum in June 2016. Investors panicked about foreign companies abandoning offices in the UK and so there was a rush to withdraw money from commercial property funds. The fund managers weren't able to give investors their cash back as they could not sell their properties at the click of a finger without accepting a massively discounted price. Many commercial property funds were forced to suspend trading until the markets had calmed down – so you couldn't take money out, or put money into these products, for a period of time.

Trading had resumed in most of the funds within four months of the referendum. Three years later, two more property funds were suspended as many investors tried to withdraw cash amid concerns about the state of the retail property market.

The events served as an important reminder about liquidity constraints that come with commercial property funds. It is worth stressing that the aforementioned fund suspensions were different to the situation with Neil Woodford's Equity Income fund discussed earlier on, as that was closed down – the property funds merely suspended dealing on a temporary basis.

Information overload

One of the challenges that a DIY investor faces is information overload. There are now more funds than there are UK equities in which to invest, and one of the main reasons for investing in funds is to make life simple.

Individual fund management firms can run many funds, each with different sub-classes and different charges. You need to make sure you invest in the right share class within a fund you have identified.

There are lots of good websites with information on funds listed at the end of the chapter and all DIY investment platforms have their own versions of these.

Costs and charges

Fund managers charge for their services like anybody else, and as an investor it is important you find out what those charges are upfront. However, it is equally important to appreciate that the lowest fees and cheapest fund may not necessarily give you the best performance. Cost and charges are therefore a factor, but not the sole factor, in helping you decide which fund you choose.

Charges and costs can come in several different forms and, to make things more complicated, different sources will refer to different parts of the costs involved in running a fund. Here are the key costs, charges and investment expenses you need to know about.

Initial charge

Some funds have historically imposed a one-off fee when you first make an investment, often in the region of 5%, to cover the cost of marketing and distribution. Today many fund companies have abolished the initial charge – or waive it for retail investors who buy funds through investment platforms or through financial advisers.

Ongoing charge

The industry has now gravitated to using the term *ongoing charges figure (OCF)* rather than its predecessors – the *annual management charge (AMC)* or *total expense ratio (TER)* – to define the annual running costs of a fund. While not perfect, this is as good an estimate as you will get and it is the figure you should use to compare fund costs.

The OCF covers the fund manager's fee and costs such as fund administration, custody, audit and regulator fees, etc.

There are still certain charges that the fund incurs that sit outside of the OCF. These additional costs include explicit costs such as dealing commissions and tax, along with implicit costs such as the bid-offer spread of underlying investments.

The industry regulator, the FCA, is continually trying to drive the fund management industry to lower costs and improve transparency, some may argue with little success.

Performance fees

Many fund managers charge performance fees, but most only do this on a select number of their funds. Performance fees are often charged as a percentage of the returns achieved above either an index, interest rate measure or other benchmark. Typically these will be 15% to 20% of a fund's returns above the target.

Managers argue that you only pay more if the fund does well. Critics point out that fund managers can get an uplift even if they deliver average performance, provided returns are above the benchmark. Furthermore, fund managers are putting themselves in a no-lose position as they suffer no penalty when their funds underperform.

Those funds that charge performance fees do so because they think they are worth it. But they have some of the highest fees in the entire fund management community. Fortunately, performance fees aren't that common, so you shouldn't have to worry about these for most mainstream funds.

Changes to the structure of funds

You can occasionally find the fund you have invested in becomes merged with another fund. This can happen if it is small and is not attracting the levels of investment the fund manager had hoped for, or if one fund manager buys another one and wants to consolidate similar funds.

You can also get the situation where funds that have become too big and unwieldy are split in two. That happened to the massively successful Fidelity Special Situations fund, which had become so big that in 2006 the manager decided to split it into two parts – a UK version and a global one.

Soft-closing of investment funds

Popular funds that generate big returns can attract floods of cash from hungry investors. But when funds get too big they can become bloated and unwieldy, unable to make the nimble investment decisions that got them their stellar performance in the first place. To stop this happening, some fund management houses like to effectively close their doors to new entrants.

Rather than simply refuse to let any new investors in at all, some sought-after fund managers *soft-close* their funds, which means they remain open but they deter new investors by putting in place punitively high initial charges to anyone wanting to make a new investment.

Multi-manager funds

If you like the idea of investing in a fund but do not want the hassle of choosing which fund managers to go for, you can always choose a fund that does all of that for you. Multi-manager funds source what they believe are the very best managers in the market, hiring and firing them whenever they believe their performance merits it. Multi-manager funds offer a one-stop shop for investors and their advisers who do not want to have to constantly revisit their fund manager selections.

But while multi-manager funds sound a great idea in theory, they introduce a whole new layer of charges into your fund management costs. You end up having to pay the multi-managers' charges as well as the charges on the funds they select, which in turn can damage your returns.

Multi-manager funds come in two distinct flavours – *fund of funds* and *manager of managers*.

Fund of funds

A fund of funds manager invests in a range of whatever unit trusts or OEICs they think will give the best return, relative to the fund's objective. Funds of funds in turn come in two types – *fettered* and *unfettered*.

Fettered funds of funds are those where the fund of funds manager can only invest in funds run by the same investment management house. This limiting of choice means the charges on fettered funds of funds are generally slightly lower, although critics say limiting the investable universe in this way goes against the grain of what a fund of funds is supposed to be all about. Unfettered funds of funds can invest in whatever funds the manager wants.

Manager of managers

Under a manager of managers structure, the fund manager instructs different investment houses to run chunks of the fund's assets on their behalf. It is a structure that works in the same way as large pension funds. Manager of managers funds create even more suspicion among investment experts than funds of funds as they are perceived as being more cumbersome.

Tax considerations for funds

Investment funds held within ISAs and SIPPs enjoy tax breaks on investments, whereas funds held outside of a tax wrapper, i.e. in a dealing account, can be liable for tax in a number of different ways.

Income from a fund is either paid as a dividend or interest, depending upon the type of fund it is.

Where it is an equity-based fund, it will pay dividends. Where it predominantly invests in cash-type instruments or bonds, such as corporate bonds or government stock known as gilts, it will pay interest.

Tax on dividend income from funds

Most funds pay income as dividends. The first £2,000 (2021/2022) you receive in dividends from investments you hold personally is tax-free every year and you can forget about tax on dividends completely for investments in a SIPP or ISA.

Once you've used up your tax-free dividend allowance, the rate you'll pay will depend on the tax band you are in.

Basic-rate taxpayers face a tax charge of 7.5% on dividend income, higher rate taxpayers must pay 32.5%, and additional rate taxpayers face a charge of 38.1%.

Tax on interest income from funds

When your fund pays interest, the personal savings allowance will apply to the taxation of interest received from unit trusts and OEICs.

This means that basic-rate taxpayers can receive up to £1,000 in interest tax-free. This reduces to £500 for higher rate and nil for additional rate taxpayers. Any excess is subject to your prevailing rate of income tax.

In general, funds that invest more in bonds pay interest, while funds that invest more in shares pay dividends.

Most individual corporate bonds and gilts pay interest gross which is taxable, unless in an ISA or SIPP, and counts towards your personal allowance.

UK corporate bond funds switched to pay interest gross in April 2017, having previously paid interest net, with 20% tax already taken.

Capital gains tax

Your fund manager doesn't pay capital gains tax on any gains made within the fund. Instead, you are taxed on any capital gains when you sell your shares or units in a fund. Capital gains tax on funds is paid at the rate of 10% if you are a basic-rate taxpayer and 20% if you are a higher or additional rate taxpayer.

ISAs and SIPPs are of course exempt from capital gains tax.

For capital gains tax purposes, funds are treated exactly like an equity, unless they are a money market or corporate or government bond fund, when most are exempt from capital gains tax.

You only pay capital gains tax on gains above your annual allowance of £12,300 (2021/2022).

Useful websites

- www.citywire.co.uk
- www.londonstockexchange.com
- www.morningstar.co.uk
- www.sharesmagazine.co.uk
- www.theinvestmentassocation.org
- www.trustnet.com

9

TRACKER FUNDS

Tracker funds, as their name suggests, track a particular investment market, usually a stock market index such as the FTSE 100, FTSE 250 or S&P 500. These funds deliver exposure to stock markets at very low cost because they do not pay fund managers to pick stocks or make big investment calls.

The active versus passive debate

One of the fiercest debates in the investment industry is whether it is actually worth paying for active fund management. In the good old days when markets were regularly delivering double-digit returns, people were less concerned at the fund manager taking 1% or 2% out of the pot for their costs.

But growing uncertainty over the state of major economies, and a widespread acceptance that developed economies are set for restrained growth for years to come, have placed an increased emphasis on charges.

This, in turn, has fuelled a growth in interest in low-cost tracker funds.

Critics of active management also argue there is so much information and analysis available on listed companies these days that we have a near-perfect market. The chances of fund managers beating the market are much slimmer than they used to be. Burden the fund manager's performance with charges and the task becomes Herculean.

Report after report has found that the majority of actively managed funds have failed to beat the index or benchmark they set themselves over a long period of time.

Supporters of active management say that while the average actively managed fund may underperform the index, high-calibre fund managers are more likely to beat it by a considerable margin.

They also say that while certain markets may be so saturated with analysis that prices are near-perfect reflections of true value, there are areas in the world where this is not the case. Emerging markets and smaller companies are good examples, where local or specialist knowledge and understanding, it is argued, are needed to interpret the data.

Active management fans also argue that tracker funds overpay for companies that are new entrants into an index and are underpaid for those companies sold when they exit an index. By constantly rebalancing to an index, you are buying the risers and selling the fallers.

The active versus passive debate divides analysts, academics, advisers and investors to this day and is not likely to be settled any time soon.

From your point of view as the DIY investor, there are merits to using both active and passive investments. Ultimately, they both provide access to the markets and help to diversify your portfolio.

Indices

The best known index in the UK is the FTSE 100. Its performance is reported daily in the national news and can be obtained from most investment platforms' websites – though often with a 15-minute delayed price.

This index tracks the share price of the 100 largest companies by value listed on the London Stock Exchange (LSE). The FTSE 250 tracks the next 250 largest companies. The FTSE All-Share index seeks to track the top 98% of companies, again by value, listed on the London Stock Exchange.

Currently, the All-Share index tracks approximately 620 of circa 2,000 companies listed in London (this figure of 2,000 includes stocks on the AIM market).

There are hundreds of indices and more are now being created to cater for the demands of passive investors. They cover all the main Investment Association sectors including equities, corporate bonds, government bonds and property, across a wide range of geographies, be they developed or emerging markets.

Increasingly you are seeing exchange-traded funds (ETFs) being developed to play big investment themes. For example, you can now get ETFs tracking the performance of companies involved in robotics, clean energy and water.

Thematic ETFs are great ways for investors to target certain areas of the market but these products will still need to attract sufficient inflows from investors to make them worth managing otherwise they might be closed down. For example, in recent years we've seen a few thematic ETFs close down including ones tracking industries involved in the whiskey and bourbon economy and companies demerged from bigger entities.

Actively managed ETFs are also starting to appear. These include products where a fund manager or a panel of experts create the criteria for the investment strategy which is then implemented in an automated way.

The structure of tracker funds

Tracker funds can take the form of a unit trust or OEIC (described in Chapter 8). If they do, they will often be available in income (INC) and accumulation (ACC) units, just like active funds.

But a large number of the new generation of tracker funds are very different in their make-up, so are worthy of individual consideration.

The new breed of tracker funds are called exchange-traded funds (ETFs), with their cousins exchange-traded commodities (ETCs) and exchange-traded notes (ETNs) completing the suite of what are collectively called exchange-traded products (ETPs). In reality, most people just use the ETF name to describe all the different types of products.

What are exchange-traded funds?

ETFs are very low-cost, passively managed funds that track indices. They have soared in popularity in recent years as canny investors realise they can track exactly the same indices they were holding in the past for a fraction of the price, with greater trading flexibility than can be offered by traditional funds.

ETFs are traded on stock exchanges like individual companies. The ETF holds a basket of equities or bonds that enable it to mimic the index it is tracking. As mentioned, ETFs are the best-known type of a group of investments known as exchange-traded products. Other ETPs include exchange-traded commodities, which track the price of commodity products like gold and oil; and exchange-traded notes, which typically track the bond markets, such as corporate bonds and gilts.

Charges on ETFs are low; they have historically been lower than those for an equivalent unit trust or OEIC tracker, but this gap has narrowed and in some cases reversed over recent years. Either way, they are normally much cheaper than actively managed funds.

They are tax efficient and they track their chosen indices fairly accurately, in fact more accurately than many unit trust or OEIC trackers. And they can be very liquid, meaning it is easy to get into and out of them at a fair price and without delay.

Similar to funds, ETFs are open-ended in nature, so price is not driven by supply and demand. The number of shares in an ETF is adjusted daily to meet the supply and demand for them.

All these factors make ETFs an attractive way for DIY investors to access a broad range of markets. ETFs are particularly suitable for charge-conscious passive investors as they keep costs down to an absolute minimum.

As with funds, not all ETFs are suitable for retail investors. Some are funds aimed at the sophisticated and high net-worth investor. One way to tell the difference is whether the term UCITS or UCIS appears in the product name, or if not on the factsheet. UCITS funds are designed for the retail investor as they are not considered complex. UCIS funds are unregulated products and higher risk as they can invest in illiquid areas like film production, forest plantations and foreign property.

There are two different structures of exchange-traded products – *physical* and *synthetic*.

Physical

A physical ETF mimics an index by holding the same investments that make up the index.

There are two main methods by which physical ETFs track an index – *full replication* and *partial replication*.

Full replication is where the ETF buys all of the assets in the index, and this is common for the more mainstream indices such as the FTSE 100. The holdings in the ETF aim to replicate exactly the holdings of the index.

Partial replication, often referred to as optimisation or sampling, is where the ETF buys the main components of an index, but not the whole of it. This may be used if the spread of the index is global, or the companies in the index are illiquid, or possibly if the ETF is small.

For an ETC tracking a commodity such as gold, physical replication would mean that the ETC physically owns the gold, albeit via a custodian. Physical replication is more common for hard commodities such as precious metals, as opposed to soft commodities such as coffee or grains such as wheat, where physical ownership of the commodity by the ETC provider is not practical.

In this instance, derivative products are used to gain synthetic exposure to the targeted commodity as opposed to owning the commodity itself.

Synthetic

A synthetic ETF involves the ETF provider entering into a contract with a financial partner called a counterparty, which is often an investment bank. This contract involves the ETF provider investing in a basket of assets, as stipulated by the counterparty, which acts as collateral.

Although this collateral must typically adhere to regulatory guidelines, it may have varying levels of correlation to the index being tracked by the ETF. The ETF provider and the counterparty then *swap* the return on the basket of assets for the return of the index: this allows the ETF provider to offer the return on the index to its investors. This is why synthetic ETFs are sometimes called *swap-based* ETFs.

Synthetic ETFs are considered riskier than physical-backed ETFs because of the counterparty risk.

They are also less likely to be a UCITS investment and hence may not be readily available to the retail DIY investor.

Tracking error

This is one of the key considerations when looking at a tracker fund, along with financial security and charges. The tracking error is the deviation of a tracker fund from the index it is tracking.

Tracking difference, or performance variation, between the fund and index is caused by charges – an index makes no allowance for charges – and also by the fact that the holdings in the tracker fund may not be identical to the index it is tracking.

Synthetic ETFs normally have the lowest tracking errors – the tracking error of a synthetic ETF is only caused by the costs associated with the underlying swap agreements. Fully replicated ETFs are the next most efficient trackers of an index and, as you may expect, partially replicated ETFs tend to have the largest deviation from their index.

The major players

There is safety in size with ETFs. Not only is a larger ETF more cost-efficient than a smaller one, but there are simply too many ETFs in the market at the moment. It does seem that professional and DIY investors have an increasing appetite for ETFs, but, nevertheless, there will be ETF closures to come, which are best avoided.

The big players are: BlackRock, which markets ETFs under the popular iShares ETFs brand; Deutsche Bank with its db X-trackers products; HSBC; Invesco; Legal & General; Société Générale with Lyxor ETFs; State Street-managed SPDR ETFs; UBS; Vanguard, the US giant whose presence in the UK is increasing rapidly; and WisdomTree.

It is a good idea to choose ETFs from these major providers.

Charges

The number one attraction of ETFs and their kind is their low cost, making them a perfect way for the cost-conscious DIY investor to get access to equity and other markets.

Charges are very low indeed. For example, Vanguard offers a FTSE 100 with an OCF of 9 basis points, or 0.09% per year.

Competition in the industry is forcing down charges which is great news for the investor. One way this is happening is through the use of lesser-known indices.

One of the biggest costs of running an ETF is licensing the index such as paying to use the FTSE or MSCI trademark. Some up and coming index providers such as Solactive have now created lower-cost indices.

For example, you can now get an ETF tracking the 100 biggest London-listed stocks for nearly half the cost of an ETF tracking the FTSE 100 and which uses that index in its name, even though you're getting exposure to the same companies.

The impact of your investment platform's costs on the total cost of ETF investing

The arrival of ultra-low-cost ETF managers in the UK has caused a bit of a stir with investment platforms.

Investment platforms have faced something of a dilemma figuring out how to charge for them. By the very nature of an ETF, it can be traded many times a day due to the large liquidity and small spreads. But equally it can be bought as a long-term hold. In the former scenario, the investment platform will earn its money from dealing commissions as it is treated like any other equity.

Where the ETF is held for a long time, the investment platform has the holding cost of the investment but no dealing income, so some level of holding or custody charge will almost certainly be made by the investment platform.

Funds and equities are often used differently by DIY investors. Funds are more likely to be held for the long term and traded infrequently, whereas equities are likely to be traded on a more regular basis. While the legal structure of an ETF is that of an equity, most DIY investors use them like a fund. Those investment platforms that charge differently for funds and equities may have a decision to make about how they charge for ETFs in the future.

Tax

ETF holdings are simply shares and so can be held within your SIPP, ISA or dealing account. They are generally treated in exactly the same way as unit trusts and OEICs for tax purposes.

You will recall that earlier in this book I pointed out the concept of bed and breakfast, where you sell a share and then buy it back again immediately to minimise your capital gains tax bill, is no longer effective.

HMRC has introduced a 30-day rule, whereby if you sell and then repurchase the same investment the transaction is ignored for capital gains tax purposes. One way around this is to hold two tracker funds in your portfolio that track the same index.

If you need to crystallise a gain or a loss, you can sell out of one tracker fund and buy the other, meaning you are not out of the market for any time and you can still manage your tax position effectively.

If you buy an ETF domiciled outside of the UK – the majority listed on the London Stock Exchange are domiciled in Ireland – there is no stamp duty. The ETF itself pays stamp duty when it buys shares, so this is consistent with how stamp duty is applied to funds.

Dividend income

Dividend income from ETFs is treated in exactly the same way as from equities and other equity funds. Your first £2,000 (2021/22) of dividend income is tax-free each year. ETFs held in an ISA or SIPP are shielded from the taxman in terms of dividend income.

Capital gains

When you sell a UK-based ETF that has increased in value it will be considered in the same way as any other share or fund for capital gains tax purposes. You don't have to pay any capital gains tax if your ETF is held in an ISA or SIPP.

Reporting status

You will find some ETFs are domiciled in countries outside the UK, such as Ireland or Luxembourg.

Most UCITS ETFs you come across as a retail investor will have a reporting status in the UK.

You can check this out on the ETF's factsheet. If the fund does have a UK reporting status its gains will be treated under capital gains tax rules. But if it does not, you might find gains are treated as income, which could lead to a far higher tax bill.

The risks associated with ETFs

The most obvious risk with an ETF is the possibility that the index or assets it is tracking will fall in value. The risk of this will reflect the underlying risk inherent in the market that the index is tracking. As you would expect, equity ETFs will be far riskier than gilt and other fixed-interest ETFs.

Tracking error is another risk and this occurs when an ETF doesn't accurately track its index. I would suggest that for most ETFs a DIY investor will use, this is unlikely to be a major issue.

Counterparty risk is an issue worrying the regulator. This is most relevant for synthetic ETFs, which are normally the preserve of the sophisticated and professional investor. Synthetic ETFs are far less common these days.

Plenty of expert investors use both sorts of ETF, but unless you feel very adventurous, stick with physical ETFs – check the factsheet before you buy to find out what backs the ETF. Providers whose ETF range is principally made up of physical ETFs include Credit Suisse, BlackRock, Invesco, UBS and Vanguard.

Small ETFs carry the risk of closure, so the answer is if you want to be on the safe side, make sure any ETF you invest in is reasonably well established and of a substantial size – I use £100m as my threshold, meaning the fund holds at least £100m in assets, but the bigger the better.

Other kinds of exchange-traded products (ETPs)

Exchange-traded products all track indices with low-cost fees, although they have slight structural differences.

Exchange-traded commodities (ETCs)

While ETFs typically track equity, bond or gilt indices, ETCs typically track commodity indices such as energy resources, metals such as gold, silver, copper and platinum, agricultural produce and livestock.

Directly accessing the investment return associated with commodities in your portfolio was very difficult for DIY investors before ETCs came along. The arrival of ETCs has allowed a new generation of investors to get access to the increases in commodity prices when these have been fuelled by demand for resources from emerging markets.

Because it is impractical to actually hold perishable commodities such as foodstuffs for any length of time, there are a large number of synthetic

ETCs in this area. As explained above, these carry some extra risks, but there is no way for a fund to track these assets other than through synthetic structures.

Exposure to commodities can be a good diversifier in an overall investment portfolio and ETCs offer an easy way to achieve this goal.

Similarly, if you want to play particular themes such as oil or metals, you can do so quickly, easily and cheaply through ETCs with exposure to these parts of the market.

Exchange-traded notes (ETNs)

ETNs are structured in a way that means they operate more like corporate or government bonds. They are not collateralised, so the investor is subject to the risk that the issuer, usually an investment bank, goes bust. This means their value is also affected by the credit rating of the bank that has issued them. The bank does not have to go bust for the investor to lose out – if the issuing bank is merely downgraded the value of an ETN can go down, even when the index they are tracking does not move at all.

With so many more straightforward trackers available on the market, DIY investors are unlikely to need to use ETNs.

The mechanics of buying and selling ETFs

Price

One advantage of ETFs over unit trusts and OEIC trackers is that they are priced continuously through the day. Unit trusts and OEICs are typically priced once a day and once you have placed an order you are never sure exactly how much you are going to pay for them. While OEICs and unit trusts are purchased at net asset value, or NAV, ETFs are typically bought and sold at a *market price*. Because ETFs are shares in companies, they are tradable whenever the market they are listed on is open.

Spread

Spreads on ETFs – the difference between the sell and the buy price – are very tight indeed. The ETFs that DIY investors are likely to want to access are massive and demand for them is never going to be a problem, which means you buy and sell for a price that is very close to the level of the underlying index.

Settlement

As with equities and funds, the settlement period is the time from the point the ETF is bought to the time the payment must be made to the selling party. The standard settlement period for ETFs is three days – this is described as T+3, T being the trading day. For the DIY investor using an investment platform, this will be largely academic as the purchase or sale of an ETF will show up on your account instantaneously.

Income

Many ETFs pay dividends, which will be paid in the same way as for other funds, such as quarterly or half-yearly. Details of income payments will be on the ETF's factsheet.

One area where a unit trust or OEIC tracker may have an advantage over an ETF is dividend reinvestment. As we saw earlier (Chapter 8), OEICs and unit trusts often have a sub-class that reinvests dividends automatically. ETFs may track an index with dividends reinvested and, if so, your dividends will be reinvested automatically. Just look for products with the term 'acc' in their name to spot dividend reinvestment ETFs. If the ETF is paying dividends to you then you may incur additional dealing and spread costs to reinvest this cash back into the market.

Stop losses and sell orders

It is possible to protect your ETF investments falling below a certain level, or bank gains once they reach a certain level, by setting up stop losses and sell orders. These are automated instructions placed through your investment platform to sell out of an ETF if its price falls to or below a certain level. These are not available for funds.

Research

ETFs are most likely to be used as a simple answer to a straightforward part of an investor's portfolio requirements – low-cost exposure to key equity and bond markets. Part of the beauty of ETFs is the fact that because they are passively managed, researching them is far less complicated than researching funds.

Once you have worked out the portfolio you want to build and decided the index or indices you want exposure to, research need not go beyond comparing the charges on different ETFs tracking that index. You may also want to check the domicile and reporting status of the ETF and decide whether to go for a synthetic or physical structure. In reality, if you are seeking to track one of the major indices, it will come down to a choice between one of the major providers, probably based on price.

Useful websites for ETFs

- www.etf.dws.com

- www.etf.com

- www.ft.com

- www.etf.hsbc.com/etf/uk/retail

- www.ishares.com/uk

- www.etf.invesco.com

- www.lyxoretf.co.uk

- www.morningstar.co.uk

- www.spdrs.com

- www.trustnet.com

- www.vanguard.co.uk

- www.wisdomtree.eu

10

INVESTMENT TRUSTS

Described by some as the City's *best-kept secret*, but attacked by critics as complex and risky, the truth about investment trusts probably lies somewhere between the two.

Investment trusts are collective investments that give you access to active management often at lower management charges than you typically pay for unit trusts and OEICs.

But these closed-ended investment vehicles do come with a level of complexity and risk that is simply not an issue for their open-ended counterparts. That said, their performance has often been better than comparable unit trusts and OEICs, making them a viable alternative for money you are looking to have professionally managed, whether for growth or income, over the medium or long term.

History

Investment trusts are the great-great-grandparents of modern OEICs and ETFs. Investment trusts you can still invest in today were among the very first collective investments the world ever saw. The first investment trust was the Foreign & Colonial Investment Trust, set up in 1868, "to give the investor of moderate means the same advantages as the large capitalists in diminishing the risk of spreading the investment over a number of stocks". Today it is still going strong under the name of F&C Investment Trust and has assets of over £4bn, giving thousands of investors access to a blend of UK and overseas equities.

Five years after the F&C Investment Trust was established, the Scottish American Investment Company started operating in Dundee, investing in railroads and government stocks. As well as being the birthplace of both *The Dandy* and *The Beano*, Dundee also gave us Alliance Trust – founded in 1878 and, more than a century later, the largest investment trust in the UK with assets of over £3bn. It is still headquartered in the same city.

These early investment trusts set up in London and Scotland started life as a means for Victorian industrialists to raise cash to finance many of the great development projects of the 19th century. Funds from these early investment trusts went towards building American railroads, establishing Malaysian rubber plantations, exploiting cattle ranches across North America and laying undersea telegraph cables between continents.

There was, however, a blot on the otherwise clean copybook of the investment industry in the early noughties, when investment trusts were very naughty.

The problems originated out of a practice investment trusts followed, whereby they were split into two share classes, with one receiving income and one receiving capital. These structures were known as split-capital trusts, or *splits* for short.

Add in the fact that these splits borrowed to *gear up* their return, while also investing in each other, and it will come as no surprise to find that disaster was just around the corner. Around 50,000 investors lost in the region of £650m when a series of splits collapsed.

But the investment trust sector is in far better shape now and controls are in place to ensure this should never be repeated.

What investment trusts can invest in

You will certainly not be stuck for choice if you want to put your money into an investment trust. There are currently more than 300 investment trusts, from generalist trusts targeting mainstream sectors for either growth or income, to niche ones targeting discrete industries such as insurance, music royalties and renewable energy.

Some investment trusts are set up with a remit of targeting specific geographical areas, from core areas such as the UK, Europe, the US and Asia Pacific, to less developed markets like those in Africa. You can also find investment trusts targeting property and cash, and at the riskier end of the spectrum those investing in hedge funds and private equity projects.

Structure

The term *trust* is confusing because investment trusts are limited companies, typically listed companies, whose business is to manage investments.

Investment trusts are collective investments that invest in different parts of the market, in the same way that unit trusts and OEICs do, with a manager making the selections on your behalf. But the difference is that there are only a fixed number of shares in each investment trust, so price changes are reflected by demand for those shares. Investment trusts are therefore closed-ended, unlike unit trusts, OEICs and ETFs, which are all open-ended.

Investment trusts are curious things. The majority of them are valued by the market as being worth less than the total value of the assets that they hold. If you have ever seen an article in the personal finance section of a newspaper about how to buy £100 worth of shares for £90, it is bound to be about investment trusts.

There are explanations aplenty for this, but none are particularly satisfactory. Why should a company with £100m of assets be valued at £90m? This is not just a temporary state of affairs – discounts have been around for nigh on 150 years.

One explanation of this difference between an investment trust's share price and the total value of its assets is that the share price is also influenced by the market's perception of the way the trust's assets are likely to perform in the future. This, in turn, is influenced by the perceived skill of the management team and the value the market believes this team can add to the trust's future performance.

To understand investment trusts, if you ever truly can, you need to understand four key factors:

1. share price

2. net asset value

3. discount

4. premium

1. Share price

Investment trusts, like all listed shares, have an offer price and a bid price, depending on whether you are buying or selling. The offer price is the price you pay when you buy the share and the bid price is the price you receive when you sell it.

Investment trusts are closed-ended vehicles, which means that the amount of shares in existence remains the same from one day to the next. Shares are normally issued only once, when an investment trust is set up, though it is possible for new shares to be issued. Like with all listed shares, the price is dictated by supply and demand.

In the case of unit trusts and OEICs, whenever you pay money to the fund manager it simply issues more units or shares and buys more assets with your cash. With investment trusts, if you buy a share in an investment trust it is not the fund manager who receives your money, but the person selling the share to you – exactly the same as if you bought a share in a company such as Tesco.

As Tesco's business performance improves, so should its share price. Investment trusts don't sell food, they manage investments; and the better they do, the higher their share price, in theory.

The market value of an investment trust is the number of shares in existence multiplied by the latest share price.

2. Net asset value (NAV)

The net asset value of an investment trust is the value of all of the assets held by the trust, less any borrowings.

The net asset value per share of the trust is the net asset value divided by the number of shares in issue; net asset value per share is also often abbreviated to NAV per share.

3. Discount

This is the odd bit. Logic should dictate that an investment trust's market value is the same as its net asset value. This is the same as saying the share price should be broadly equal to its net asset value per share. But this isn't the case, and the difference between the two is known as the discount or premium.

In most cases, investment trusts' share prices are lower than their net asset value per share. If this is the case, the trust is said to be trading at a discount. If a trust has a share price of 90p and its NAV per share is 100p, it is said to be trading at a 10% discount.

In early 2021, approximately 70% of investment trusts were trading at a discount to NAV.

Movements in discounts, which can narrow or widen significantly, can have a greater influence on the investment return you get from your investment trust holding than the actual performance of the underlying investments.

Some people argue that if you are investing for a long time you can ignore the discount because the difference it will make to the overall total return will be marginal. If you buy at a 10% discount and sell later at a 10% discount, then the fact there was a discount has had no effect on your return. The quality of the fund manager and the consistency of its performance will be more important.

But discounts can be very volatile over the short term and may undergo a structural shift over the long term. Take the F&C Commercial Property

Trust. It was trading at a 40% discount in late 2008. Theoretically that meant by investing in it you were buying £100 worth of UK commercial property for £60. That suggests that the market did not believe the investment trust's valuation of its assets. Within a year, it was trading at a 15% premium.

It is not hard to accept a discount or premium on a commercial property investment trust as the valuations of commercial property are open to judgement and can often lag the market. But these discounts also exist on equity-based investment trusts that do not face the same liquidity and valuation challenges.

One conclusion you may reach when looking at a discount for an investment trust is that the market is ascribing a negative value to the fund management team that is managing the fund. The market is saying that the investment trust is worth more wound up than it is if it carries on.

So why aren't all investment trusts that trade at a discount wound up? Good question. In reality, if the market thought that an investment trust had a realistic prospect of winding up, its discount would narrow. What typically happens is that the managers of an investment trust can narrow its discount by buying its own shares in the market, and many investment trusts do this.

Some will argue that a large discount on an investment trust is a buying opportunity, but I would suggest that, in itself, the level of a discount shouldn't be a sufficient justification to buy. There will be a reason why the market has placed a high discount on an investment trust and the market will always know more than you. Until you know why a discount exists, you cannot make a call as to whether it will widen or narrow.

These fluctuations in discounts can give investors either fabulous or terrible returns depending on which side of the deal they are on. They also show how investment trusts are heavily dependent on market sentiment. If things go well, you do very well, but if markets turn sour, you can get the double whammy of a falling NAV compounded by a widening discount.

4. Premium

While the majority of investment trusts trade at a discount, some actually trade at a premium, which means the investment trust is valued at more than the total value of the assets it owns.

This is the flip side of a discount. It may represent the high demand for the services of the management team, it may reflect the fact that an investment trust is investing in an area desired by investors but which is very difficult to access, or it may be that the net asset value understates how much the investment trust is really worth.

I would urge extreme caution if you are buying an investment trust at a premium. As with buying one at a discount, you should try and understand why the premium exists before investing.

Nick Train, manager of the top-performing Lindsell Train Investment Trust, has told investors on many occasions over the past half-decade or more not to buy his investment trust because it was too expensive.

Lindsell Train Investment Trust was trading at an astonishing 85% premium to NAV in mid-2019. One argument is that the investment trust owns a large stake in the management company that runs several funds, including Lindsell Train, and this investment is grossly undervalued in the trust's accounts.

Borrowing/gearing

Unlike unit trusts and OEICs, investment trusts are allowed to borrow money to gear their investments. The amount of borrowing, or gearing, that an investment trust is allowed is prescribed by the investment trust itself. Usually they allow borrowing of around 10% of the investment trust's market capital. This amplifies returns, either good or bad, which is why investment trusts often perform better than unit trusts and OEICs in rising markets and worse in falling ones.

You can find out how much gearing an investment trust has at the Association of Investment Companies website. Like other types of fund, you will find that investment trusts have factsheets that contain key information about them and these can be obtained from websites such as Morningstar or Trustnet.

The idea is that the investment trust manager will gear up the investment trust when they think there are good opportunities and reduce borrowing in more difficult times. It's a way for the manager to be able to put their foot on the gas if they think there are fantastic opportunities in the market.

Risks

Investment trusts are risky investments in the same way that most unit trusts, OEICs and ETFs are risky – they are able to invest in equities, property and other assets whose price can go down as well as up. The fact that these collective investments put money into lots of different assets means risk is lower than direct investment into single company shares.

Investment trusts are riskier than unit trusts and OEICs in part because they are able to borrow money to increase potential returns.

But demand for the investment trust itself can also fluctuate. For example, around the time of the split-cap investment trust debacle, sentiment towards investment trusts was relatively negative, and was reflected in wider discounts. As it happened, this presented investors with a great investment opportunity – as faith was subsequently restored to the market and discounts narrowed.

The risks of investment trusts should not be overstated. They are still a viable alternative to actively managed unit trusts and OEICs and have, over most sectors and criteria, performed better than them.

Split-cap trusts, warrants, real estate investment trusts and venture capital trusts all carry their own special risks, which are explained below.

Performance

Investment trusts have been beating their open-ended counterparts for years, in part because of their lower management costs. For instance, a report by AJ Bell in July 2019 found that in 75% of cases an investment trust outperformed an open-ended fund run by the same manager over a ten-year period. This makes investment trusts an attractive alternative to actively managed unit trusts and OEICs for those willing to accept the additional risks associated with gearing and discounts.

Charges

For years the investment trust community has trumpeted the lower charges levied by closed-ended funds compared to unit trusts and OEICs, and rightly so. But with the banning of commissions payable to advisers, the charges for funds – unit trusts and OEICs – are now more on a par with investment trusts.

It's also worth being aware that performance fees are more common among investment trusts than they are in the unit trust and OEIC world, with 31% of investment trusts charging performance fees typically of up to 20% of outperformance of a predetermined benchmark, as of the start of 2020.

If minimising charges is your primary objective then it may be that passive funds such as ETFs are more suitable. But if you want actively managed pooled investments, investment trusts are an affordable option, if you can get your head around some of the additional complexities.

You should be able to find most of the information you need on a trust's own website in order to carry out a comparison of charges.

Research

There are plenty of specialist investment trust teams within broker organisations that produce reams of material on whom they think are the good and bad managers – see the websites at the end of this chapter.

Both Trustnet and Morningstar have a lot of easy-to-access information on investment trusts, including historic data on share price, net asset value, structure and analytics, allowing you to compare different investment trusts across a range of criteria. Morningstar and Citywire give regular commentary on what is going on in the investment trust sector.

When researching investment trust managers, you should take a similar approach to researching unit trust and OEIC fund managers. Look at independent sources such as *Shares* magazine and *Investors Chronicle*, explore Trustnet and Morningstar, read the financial press and browse the investment trust's website.

You want to look for managers with a track record of at least three years' decent performance. Always consider the NAV per share as much as the share price and – for income-generating trusts – make sure the trust has not had to eat into its capital to maintain its dividend.

Given so much of the value of an investment trust is down to sentiment, it is also worth gauging the mood for or against a particular trust around the various internet sites commenting on the sector, as this will ultimately be reflected in discounts and premiums.

Avoid anything trading at a huge premium or discount unless you are absolutely convinced of the fundamentals – it may be trading at such a large discount because the market knows something about it that you don't.

Corporate actions

Occasionally you will get mergers or takeovers of investment trusts, particularly where small operations are failing to achieve critical mass and can benefit from the economies of scale that being part of a bigger organisation will offer.

Small investment trusts may be targets if the management is not doing very well or because costs make up a disproportionately large part of the fund's assets, so being acquired by a bigger player is probably no bad thing from the shareholders' perspective.

If you hold shares in the investment trust making the acquisition, chances are you will not be offered anything as part of the deal. Beyond exercising your shareholder vote, you will have little say in what happens.

While the number of investment trust shares in existence does not change from day to day, new shares can be issued, just as for any limited company, which has the impact of raising new funds for the company to manage.

It must be noted that investment trusts do benefit from having an independent board of directors, which isn't the case for open-ended funds. The board's job is to ensure the fund manager fulfils their mandate and acts in the best interest of shareholders. They have the power to sack the fund manager if they feel performance is unacceptable and there are plenty of examples of boards doing this – or threatening to do so – in recent years.

Dividends

Investment trusts can be used for growth or income, in the same way that other investment funds can. Some income investment trusts have very high yields indeed.

Unlike unit trusts and OEICs, investment trusts have the ability to retain income in revenue reserves, which means they can hold money back in good years so they can maintain their dividend payment in leaner ones. Unit trusts and OEICs are obliged to distribute the income they receive every year.

Growth investment trusts will hope to use this mechanism to steadily grow their dividend year after year. For example, in 2019 Janus Henderson's City of London Investment Trust could boast a record of increasing its dividend every year for over half a century.

The mechanics of buying and selling investment trusts

As previously stated, despite their name, investment trusts are not trusts but limited companies. As such, when you buy or sell your holding, you are simply buying or selling an amount of shares in a company. The mechanics of doing this are the same as buying and selling any other shares through your investment platform, although it is worth noting that some investment trust shares can have liquidity problems.

As with the purchase of other shares, you will have to pay stamp duty of 0.5% on the purchase of shares in an investment trust. If the purchase is over £10,000 in value you have to pay the £1 Panel of Mergers and Takeovers levy as well, which applies to all equity purchases.

In addition to stamp duty you will also have to pay your investment platform's dealing commission when you buy and sell. You will recall that when you buy a unit trust, an OEIC or an ETF, you don't pay stamp duty as the fund pays stamp duty on all the shares it buys. There is no such exemption for investment trusts. You pay stamp duty when you buy a share in an investment trust and the investment trust also pays stamp duty when it buys shares as an investment, which seems somewhat inconsistent, but that's the way it is.

Unit trusts and OEICs have grown with the retail investor in mind, particularly those who don't have much money to invest. Hence we have seen the growth of income and accumulation units – regular premium investing is part of their DNA.

Investment trusts, like ETFs, are more akin to equities in that they are slightly more grown up and you may not find it quite as easy, or cost-effective, to reinvest dividends from an ETF or investment trust as you would from an OEIC or a unit trust.

However, most investment platforms offer a dividend reinvestment facility for shares including ETFs and investment trusts, typically charging £1.50 per transaction – so straightforward dividend reinvestment is certainly not out of the question.

Spread/liquidity

As with any other traded share, the spread on the share price of an investment trust is the difference between the bid price and the offer price. Spreads are set by market makers and their size will depend on liquidity.

This liquidity issue is not a problem for unit trusts and OEICs, where units are created or cancelled to meet demand. When you sell a small stake in an investment trust, there will usually be a market waiting to take them off your hands. But large orders may face liquidity problems.

What amounts to large will depend on the trust. There is usually no trouble offloading £50,000 stakes in the bigger investment trusts, but for some smaller ones, £5,000 or £10,000-worth can be problematic.

You can check how much the market says it will take off your hands at more or less the price being quoted on the screens by looking at the exchange market size (EMS) – which is quoted on the 'Prices & Markets' section of the London Stock Exchange website (www.londonstockexchange.com).

The EMS is the number of shares in the investment trust that you can safely expect to be able to trade without the spread widening significantly. You can normally trade up to three times the EMS figure without facing any problems, although in volatile market conditions only the EMS may be available.

Attempt to buy or sell even £10,000-worth of shares in a less well-known investment trust automatically through your investment platform and it is unlikely you will be able to place the deal online. You will be asked to ring up your investment platform to place the deal and it is likely that you will get a less favourable price than the price on your screen.

Settlement period

We discussed the challenges of switching between funds earlier in this book, in particular the problem with the fact that you will be out of the market for a day or more if you want to sell a fund and then use the proceeds to buy another fund.

You don't have this problem with investment trusts, as your account will be notionally credited immediately when you sell an investment trust and you can use these funds to buy another investment, there and then. As with most equities, settlement is normally T+3.

Special types of investment trust holdings

Split-capital trusts

Split-capital trusts, also referred to as *split-cap trusts* or *splits*, are a special sort of investment trust that issues different classes of shares that pays out returns to their different classes of shareholders in different ways. They also differ from mainstream investment trusts in that most have a set winding-up date.

Investment trusts, on the other hand, generally only have one class of share and the performance of the trust is only reflected in the dividends and the share price.

The idea behind creating different classes of shares is that it enables the trust to better meet the needs of different types of shareholders. For example, a simple split-capital trust might issue income shares and growth or *zero* shares, with the income shareholders getting all of the income and capital shareholders getting all the capital growth.

The split-cap debacle

Just because zero dividend preference shares are supposed to pay out a fixed sum, this does not mean they always do. Over 50,000 investors discovered this at their own cost in 2000 and 2001 when a whole raft of split-cap trusts collapsed, leaving zero holders with next to nothing.

As is so often the case, the problem stemmed from a lack of understanding of the risks the products held, which in the case of the split-cap debacle was compounded by aggressive marketing that skated over these risks. At the end of the 1990s some brokers were pushing zeros as low-risk investments that had never failed in the past.

When markets then plummeted in 2000 many split-cap trusts collapsed, leaving zero and income shares worth just a few pence in the pound, or in some cases nothing at all. Investors suffered combined losses in the region of £650m.

It emerged that split-cap trusts had been investing in each other, a revelation that sparked allegations of a magic circle of managers buying each other's trusts to keep their asset prices from falling.

The regulatory bodies intervened and investigated, although never published their findings of exactly what had gone on. But fund managers and brokers were forced to pay hundreds of millions of pounds in compensation. Since then, split-cap trusts' reputation has slowly recovered and respectable names have continued to launch new ones since then. Even so, splits remain a niche product for real experts, and DIY investors will want to approach them with caution.

Real estate investment trusts (REITs)

A real estate investment trust (REIT) is a company listed on the stock exchange that makes money by buying, selling and renting properties. A REIT, which is pronounced *reet*, has the same structure as an investment trust in that it is closed-ended, so does not issue new shares to match supply and demand for its shares. Instead, as with other investment trusts, the price of the shares goes up or down depending on the demand for them, in turn reflecting both the value of the underlying asset and the market's perception of the prospects for the sector.

REITs can invest in both commercial and residential property. Until the launch of a brace of residential property OEICs in 2012, REITs had been the only way to hold residential property assets in your SIPP.

REITs originated in the USA in 1960 when they were introduced as a structure that would reduce or eliminate corporation tax in real estate investment companies. But they were not introduced in the UK until 2007, at which time nine UK property companies, including British Land, Land Securities and Liberty International, converted to REIT status.

To qualify as a REIT, the company has to distribute at least 90% of its income as dividends. That makes them very appealing to investors wanting to generate an income from the market and possibly use regular dividend payments to help pay their household bills.

Liquidity

Spreads on REITs will widen at times in the economic cycle when the property they hold, be it commercial or residential or a combination of both, is out of favour. But at least you will always be able to sell your stake in a REIT for whatever the market really thinks it is worth.

This is not always the case with open-ended vehicles such as commercial property unit trusts and OEICs, which have the power to close their doors in the event that prices fall, so they do not have to offload their property holdings in a fire sale if investors demand their money.

In this situation, dealing in the fund would be suspended temporarily and investors would not be able to buy or sell, such as happened in 2016 following the EU referendum result and in 2019 when a few shopping centre-focused REITs saw large investor sell orders.

Investment trusts – tax rules and considerations

These are broadly the same as for equities. Investment trusts can be held within ISAs, SIPPs and dealing accounts. You don't pay tax on dividends on investments held in an ISA or SIPP.

For anything held in a dealing account, you don't pay tax on the first £2,000 (2021/22) of dividends that you get in the tax year, which runs from 6 April to 5 April.

Above this allowance, the tax you pay depends on which income tax band you're in. You need to add your income from dividends to your other taxable items when working this amount out. You may pay tax at more than one rate.

Basic-rate taxpayers will pay 7.5% on dividends over the tax-free dividend allowance. Higher rate taxpayers will pay 32.5% and the additional rate level is 38.1%.

Non-UK dividend income is normally received net of local withholding taxes. Some credit may be given for tax already paid if the UK has a double taxation agreement in place with the country where that dividend income is generated.

Investment trusts do not pay capital gains tax themselves, similar to unit trusts and OEICs. Instead the gains are taxed in the hands of the investor, after their capital gains tax allowance has been used up.

Venture capital trusts

Tax-free income, tax-free capital growth and 30% tax relief on the way in are the bait used to try to get you to take on the risk of investing in early-stage companies. To access these attractive benefits you have to put your faith in venture capital trusts (VCTs).

With the lower limits on contributions into pensions starting to bite and the top rate of tax at 45%, interest in VCTs among wealthier investors is growing. For less wealthy DIY investors, on the other hand, VCTs are likely to remain off the spectrum.

VCTs are a specialist form of investment trust given generous tax advantages to encourage investment in small businesses at an early stage in their expansion. You invest in the VCT and the VCT invests in the underlying start-up companies. They are a way for companies not big enough to be listed on a stock exchange to get access to funds.

For investors to be able to claim tax breaks, the VCT's assets have to be invested in qualifying companies – small companies that carry out a qualifying trade. *Small* in this case is a company with less than £15m of gross assets on its balance sheet and it may be unquoted or possibly listed on one of the junior stock exchanges, such as the Alternative Investment Market (AIM). Non-qualifying trades include farming, property development and professional services.

The main tax relief measures are only available to those who subscribe for the initial shares. The shares in the VCT are typically listed on a stock exchange, yet you wouldn't qualify for the 30% tax relief if you bought in the secondary market.

Without the tax advantages, many DIY investors would probably not want to invest in the companies that a VCT invests in. A large degree of faith in the expertise of the managers who run them is needed. But the generous tax advantages they offer can make them a useful tax-planning tool. And if you are an experienced DIY investor, understand the risks and wait for opportunities to materialise, you can find corners of the VCT market that offer good value and that will deliver decent returns.

Tax relief on VCTs

The tax relief you get on VCTs depends on whether you are an original investor or you bought the shares on the secondary market via the stock exchange.

The relief on newly issued VCT shares includes:

- Exemption from income tax on dividends on ordinary shares.

- Exemption from capital gains tax on disposal of shares.

- You can invest up to £200,000 each year with income tax relief at 30% for subscriptions of new shares, provided the shares are held for at least five years – tax relief is limited to the amount of income tax you pay.

The relief on VCT shares bought on the secondary market includes:

- Exemption from income tax on dividends on ordinary shares.

- Exemption from capital gains tax on disposal of shares.

If you buy VCTs on the secondary market, there is no 30% income tax relief on your investment but this does count towards your £200,000 limit.

VCTs for income

The tax-free income from VCTs can make them attractive for DIY investors paying tax at 40% or 45%, provided you find the right ones. For a 40% taxpayer, a 6% yield from a VCT is equivalent to a 10% yield from income that is not subject to tax relief.

When looking for VCTs for income, focus on past net asset value returns more than share price. You should also look out for VCTs that have shown they can maintain payouts at a decent level without eating into their net asset value per share.

You do not get the 30% tax relief on the secondary market, but that does not mean there are not bargains to be found, and you do not have to worry about holding them for five years to benefit from the tax-free income and gains.

VCTs can be specialist, meaning they target a particular sector such as healthcare and biotech, technology or the environment, or generalist, meaning managers can invest in a broad range of companies. In practice, most VCTs these days are generalist.

Early bird discounts on VCT shares

It is worth getting in early if you are going for new VCT shares. Many people invest in VCTs as the end of the tax year approaches, in February or March, yet launches usually start in November, with some even open for subscription in September.

To help build momentum behind their launch many VCTs offer early bird incentives, normally a small reduction in the initial fee. There is always the risk that the VCT won't achieve critical mass and the launch doesn't go ahead, in which case your money is returned to you. On the other hand, leave it too late and you can find the VCT you want reaches capacity early and closes before you get in.

But VCTs are by no means plain sailing. The companies they invest in are notoriously risky and charges are much higher than other investment trusts and funds – often well in excess of 2%.

What's more, when you come to sell, liquidity can be poor, meaning you may struggle to find someone to buy your shares. For this reason, when buying and selling VCT shares, however big or small the holding, it is always worth getting on the phone to your investment platform to get them to see how the land lies. Try to sell them online and you may get a poor deal.

That said, there are a few VCT providers, such as Octopus Investments, which now buy shares directly from the investor when they want to sell.

Useful websites

- www.sharesmagazine.co.uk
- www.londonstockexchange.com
- www.morningstar.co.uk
- www.bpf.org.uk/reits-and-property-companies
- www.theaic.co.uk
- www.citywire.co.uk
- www.trustnet.com

11

EQUITIES (STOCKS AND SHARES)

E quities are likely to be the driving force behind many DIY investors' portfolios. They can be held directly through an ISA, SIPP or dealing account, or indirectly through funds run by professional managers.

Yes, their value can go down as well as up, but since the 19th century equities have outperformed pretty much every other regularly traded asset class by a country mile.

The word *equities* is interchangeable with *stocks* and *shares*, and covers all the different types of shares in a company that an investor can buy, hold and sell. A limited company's owners are its shareholders, so when you buy shares you become a part-owner of the company.

Investors can profit from holding shares in two ways – when the company pays a dividend and when the value of its shares increases.

The history of equities

The rise of equities over the last few centuries pretty much tracks the growth of the capitalist economic system. The concept of ownership of a profit-making organisation being divided up into tradable shares first appeared back in Roman times.

Arguably the first recognisable limited company was the East India Company. It was set up in 1600 under a charter granted by Elizabeth I that gave it trading privileges in India. Two years later, the Dutch East India Company issued shares on the newly created Amsterdam Stock Exchange. The concept of the limited company, with individuals' legal liability for any debts or other losses created by the company limited to their investment in the shares, coupled with the ability to pool thousands of investors into a single project, fuelled much of the economic growth in Europe and the United States through the following centuries.

Until 30-odd years ago, share ownership was pretty much the preserve of wealthy individuals. But the privatisations and demutualisations of the 1980s and 1990s saw millions of individuals become shareholders for the very first time.

More recently, high profile stock market flotations such as Royal Mail have also attracted a new audience to investing in individual shares. A long period of low interest rates has also pushed more people towards equities as a source of income.

Furthermore, schemes offering employees shares in the company for whom they work have also increased share ownership, while the growth of the internet has seen the cost of buying equities fall, cutting out the need for an old-school stockbroker.

A bumpy ride

Europe and America's economies have been on an upward trend for many decades now and equity investors have benefited from the ride. But it hasn't all been plain sailing. In fact, history shows us stock markets have crashed with depressing regularity.

One of economic historians' favourite crashes, if you can have such a thing, is the so-called South Sea Bubble of 1720. Stock in the South Sea Company, a British company with the rights to exploit parts of South and Central America, started a seemingly inexorable rise from £100 a share to almost £1,000 in a matter of just a few months. Blinded by greed, investors rich and poor ploughed their savings into what they believed was a one-way bet, without regard to the fact that the territories the company held the rights to exploit were all controlled by Spain, with whom Britain was at war.

When promised dividends didn't materialise, investors started running for the door and the shares were decimated, falling back down to £100 again by the end of the year. And it wasn't just stupid people who lost money – Sir Isaac Newton is said to have lost today's equivalent of £2.4m in the company.

The 19th and 20th centuries have also had their fair share of market collapses, with the Wall Street Crash of 1929 perhaps the most famous of them all, kicking off the Great Depression of the 1930s.

Within living memory for anyone over the age of 50 is the crash of 1973 and 1974, which was caused by the devaluation of the US dollar and a spike in the price of oil. The UK fared worse than most in that crash, with the FT30, then the leading index in this country, falling 73% top to bottom.

Since then we have lived through 1987's Black Monday, 1992's Black Wednesday, 1997's Asian Crisis, 1998's Russian Crisis, 2000's dot-com bubble, the 9/11 market falls and the 2002 downturn, among others. Then, of course, there was the credit crunch of 2008, kicked off by the collapse of Lehman Brothers, which triggered the global financial crisis that developed economies are still struggling to extricate themselves from to this day.

The EU referendum result in June 2016 caused another stock market crash, albeit only very temporarily as the FTSE 100 blue-chip index ended that year on a record high.

The coronavirus pandemic caused a collapse in global markets at the start of 2020. Share prices fell nearly across the board, commodity prices including oil were badly hit and the pound took a beating.

It is fairly certain there will be more stock market wobbles in the future. But don't let that put you off.

Easy to say, you might think, but with all that bad news, why would anyone want to invest in equities? Because equities are still expected to do what they have done for long-term investors ever since the 19th century – perform better than other asset classes.

Barclays has been comparing the performance of equities, cash on deposit and gilts (UK government bonds) for over half a century, with performance comparisons going back to 1899. The 2019 edition of its annual *Equity Gilt Study* showed that equities have outperformed gilts and cash on deposit for much of that 119-year period. The sum of £100 invested in equities back in 1899 would, with dividends reinvested, have grown to £2,706,467 by the end of 2018. If you had put your money into cash, it would have grown to just £20,733.

Equities can have sustained periods when they do not deliver – the first decade of the new millennium has been described as the 'lost decade for equities' because returns were lower than bonds and cash over the period. However, equities have almost always delivered the goods over the long term. Looking at ten-year consecutive periods since 1899, equities have outperformed cash in a ratio of nine to one.

Of course equities can be volatile, which is why you might not want your whole portfolio in them. And there is no guarantee that equities are going to make you rich quickly. But over the long term they can deliver returns that you will not be able to get at the bank or building society.

The different types of equity

Ordinary shares

These are the mainstream shares typically held by equity investors. An ordinary share is anything that is not a preference or convertible share. The vast majority of equities that a DIY investor holds will be of this type.

Preference shares

Preference shares are a special class of share that pay investors a fixed dividend, making them typically of interest to investors looking for steady returns. That said, they are considerably less common today than they were a decade ago.

Dividends on ordinary shares are not guaranteed, as investors in BP found in 2010 when the oil giant cut its dividend altogether following the Gulf of Mexico disaster, and again in 2020 when the coronavirus caused many companies to suspend dividends and use that cash to help keep their business going. Dividends on preference shares, on the other hand, are fixed. But if the company does not have the cash to pay it in any one year, they accrue until it does.

Unlike ordinary shares, preference shares do not normally entitle the holder to a vote, unless the dividend has not been paid.

Preference shares rank higher than ordinary shares in the event that a company goes into liquidation but they rank behind bank creditors on the winding-up of a company. In practice this protection should not be overstated, as preference shareholders often get little or no money back in the event of a company's insolvency.

Convertibles

Convertible preference shares are a form of preference share that also gives the investor a predetermined dividend with the option to convert them into ordinary shares in the event their price reaches a fixed price at a later date.

Companies use them as a way to raise cash more cheaply than bonds because the option to convert later is deemed to be of value, meaning they can offer investors a bit less income up front. The option price is usually set considerably higher than the share's current price.

The benefit for the investor is that they have the security of knowing they will get a certain dividend come what may, with the added flexibility that if the company starts to do really well and pays an even higher dividend than that paid by the convertible, the holder can convert and benefit from it, provided the share price has risen to the option price.

If the convertible never makes up that ground on the option price it is known as a *busted convertible* and will be valued in a similar way to a bond. However, as it approaches or exceeds the conversion price, its value will increasingly correlate with the value of the stock itself, because the chance of conversion becomes more likely.

Where to invest – markets, sectors and indices

Modern investment platforms and brokers give you ready access to a bewildering array of investment markets around the globe. But unless you are an experienced stock picker, most of the stocks you are likely to hold will be listed in the UK.

Companies can be classified on basis of size, the index under which they are listed, the sector or industry they operate in, or the geographical region in which they trade. With so many companies out there, filtering companies on this basis can guide you towards the sorts of stocks that are right for you.

The London Stock Exchange (LSE)

The London Stock Exchange is the fourth-largest stock exchange in the world, and the largest in Europe. Founded in 1801 and now based near St Paul's Cathedral, it is open for trading between 08.00hrs and 16.30hrs, Monday to Friday, excluding bank holidays. Its main market lists the shares of over 700 companies from around the world.

The LSE also houses the Alternative Investment Market, called AIM for short. AIM shares can be held in your SIPP, ISA or dealing account.

FTSE 100

Everyone has heard of the FTSE. Pronounced *Footsie*, originally it stood for Financial Times Stock Exchange.

The FTSE 100 index is the one you constantly hear referred to on the news and in the papers. It reflects the average weighted share price of the 100 largest stocks on the LSE. For most mainstream indices, including the FTSE 100, size means market capitalisation (market cap), or value. The 100 largest companies are thus the 100 most valuable companies. The movement of the FTSE is influenced by its very biggest constituents which include oil producers and banks. They are so much larger in size than many of the stocks in the index so when they rise, the index rises. When they fall, the index is also probably going to fall.

FTSE 100 companies are the giants of economies in different parts of the world including the UK. Their combined share value represents more than two-fifths of the entire value of all the quoted shares in the UK. FTSE 100 companies are generally mature companies that should be less volatile than smaller companies.

The FTSE 100 was established in 1984, with a base price of 1,000. It reached 6,950 on the penultimate trading day of the last millennium, 30 December 1999. The post-credit crunch gloom took it to below 3,500 in March 2009. Fast forward to May 2018 and the FTSE 100 was trading at new record highs of approximately 7,778.

It is worth remembering that the FTSE index reflects only the values of the companies' shares and not the income generated through the payment of dividends. So if, for example, the FTSE 100 stayed at 6,000 for a year, that does not mean investors would have made nothing at all over that period, as they would have received the dividends paid. The average dividend yield – the dividend expressed as a percentage of the price – of the FTSE 100 has typically been between 3% and 5% over recent years. Some pay dividends well in excess of this average, but of course some companies also pay less.

The index includes household names such as Vodafone, Tesco and Unilever, as well as banks, tobacco and pharmaceutical companies and oil producers. But just because FTSE 100 companies are listed on the LSE, it doesn't mean they are British companies through and through. Companies do not have to be based in the UK to get a listing on the LSE, they just need to trade their shares in London.

Wind the clock back 20 years and the FTSE 100 pretty much reflected the UK economy and its trading overseas. Today things are very different. Fizzy drink bottling group Coca Cola HBC and miner Anglo American are just two examples of the numerous companies whose core businesses are conducted predominantly outside the UK, but which are included in the FTSE 100.

Overseas companies listed on the LSE can give you great returns, but they are often commodity plays and you should not think they are similar in profile to steady consumer goods or utilities stocks just because they are in the FTSE 100.

These overseas companies like being listed on the LSE because it gives them kudos and demonstrates a certain level of governance. It also means that once they become a FTSE 100 constituent, a certain level of demand for their shares will be supported by investment houses running trackers following the index unless, that is, their price falls so sharply that they drop out of the index.

FTSE 250 (mid-cap stocks)

If you want to go for growth in your portfolio and are comfortable with some risk, a good place to start is the FTSE 250.

The FTSE 250 is the next tier below the FTSE 100, covering the 101st to 350th largest companies quoted in the UK.

Stocks in the FTSE 250 are generally described as mid-cap companies, which broadly means they are worth between £400m and £4bn. Promotion and demotion between higher and lower indices happens on a quarterly basis, so recently ejected former FTSE 100 stocks find their way into this index, and companies promoted from the FTSE 250 head into the FTSE 100.

Because they are smaller than FTSE 100 companies, FTSE 250 companies tend to have more scope for growth. It goes without saying that it is a lot easier for a company with a market cap of £400m to double in size than, say, HSBC with a market cap of almost £100bn. Property website Rightmove is a good example of a FTSE 250 success story, its shares growing in value by over 700% in the ten years to the start of 2021.

But these companies can also be less stable than FTSE 100 companies. Income seekers will generally do better with FTSE 100 shares as FTSE 250 companies tend to pay lower dividends, although there are some exceptions.

Mid-cap stocks theoretically reflect the UK economy more closely than the FTSE 100, which has a large global bias through its constituent companies. That said, FTSE 250 companies are themselves becoming increasingly global, with around half having overseas revenues. Both the FTSE 100 and 250 contain investment trusts, which are basically funds set up as limited companies that invest in other shares.

Supporters of mid-cap investments argue that they offer a greater choice than large-cap companies, which are dominated by whatever the theme of the moment is – banks and insurance companies one year and oil, gas and mining companies the next. Less risky than small-cap stocks and more nimble than blue-chips, the FTSE 250 should be the ideal hunting ground for the experienced stock-picker.

Recent history has actually turned the conventional wisdom that large-caps do better in tough market conditions on its head. In the ten years to the start of January 2021, the FTSE 100 rose 9.5%. The FTSE 250, meanwhile, rose more than eight times as much at 77%. That said, in times of market stress, mid-caps are likely to be more volatile.

FTSE 350

Rarely followed as an index, the FTSE 350 is simply the 350 largest companies on the LSE, and is an amalgamation of the FTSE 100 and FTSE 250.

FTSE SmallCap

Companies listed on the FTSE that are not in the FTSE 100 or FTSE 250, and are not on AIM (see below), are listed on either the FTSE SmallCap or Fledgling index. They are typically companies with a market cap of less than £200m. The FTSE SmallCap is considered to be the more important of the two.

Small-cap companies are, by their very nature, more volatile than bigger ones, meaning you should only invest in them if you can afford to lose some or all of your money. On the other hand, they can deliver spectacular growth if you choose the right ones.

Their very volatility can make small-cap companies an attractive target if you are looking to deal regularly. If a company performs badly for a long period of time, unhappy investors will tend to sell out of the stock. Management should eventually take note of this and make positive changes, and provided the company's basic proposition has not been undermined by external factors, canny investors can eke out decent returns.

That said, spreads (explained in more detail below) can be wide, making high turnover of shares an expensive business.

Studies have suggested that small-cap companies tend to perform better coming out of an economic downturn, but lag at other times. However, the wide variety of companies that make up the FTSE SmallCap means that some will do the exact opposite.

There are also a lot of investment trusts in the index – Janus Henderson has six investment trusts listed in the FTSE SmallCap and BlackRock has five trusts in the index.

The Alternative Investment Market (AIM)

AIM is the LSE's market for smaller companies, including early-stage businesses and those backed by venture capital. It now lists around 840 small companies, many of whom are overseas companies.

AIM has less rigorous reporting standards than the main LSE market, allowing smaller companies the flexibility to float on a recognised exchange, but without the high accountancy and legal costs associated with a full listing. There are also no capital requirements for companies and they come with tax breaks for investors.

Tax breaks for AIM shares

A large number of shares held on AIM become exempt from inheritance tax once they have been held for two years, making them a potential estate-planning tool, although the downside is that the volatility associated with them makes them generally less suitable for investors approaching the end of their life.

Investing in AIM companies

AIM companies are all about growth – not dividends – and liquidity is even more of an issue in AIM than it is in the FTSE SmallCap. They are more volatile and hence riskier than companies listed on the main market.

Overseas stock markets

You can invest in most of the major stock exchanges around the world through your investment platform, with most overseas blue-chip companies eligible for ISA and SIPP investment. The majority of mainstream shares can be traded online, provided the market is open in that country, although some will need to be traded over the telephone.

There is no 0.5% stamp duty on overseas equities, although some markets may have their own levies.

When you buy overseas equities, your investment platform will convert the sterling in your account into the currency of the country in which you are buying the shares.

Why buy overseas equities?

DIY investors tend to stick with UK equities, in part because it is a market we are closer to and understand better. But there is nothing wrong with putting your money in overseas equities, whether it is well-known names such as Apple, BMW or Coca Cola, or fast-maturing companies in developing nations.

In fact, investing overseas will not only give you access to some of the world's dynamic manufacturing and commodity-based economies, it will also help dampen down volatility in your overall portfolio. This is because different economies around the world are rarely at the same place in the investment cycle at exactly the same time.

But there are risks to investing overseas, the most obvious one being currency risk. If US shares in your portfolio rise by 20%, but the dollar depreciates 20% against sterling, then you have made nothing. Worse still is if both your US shares and the dollar fall 20%, in which case you can end up seriously out of pocket.

When it comes to emerging markets, while they may be more volatile in the short term, the conventional wisdom is that developing economies' currencies are likely to strengthen against sterling in the coming decades, meaning UK investors will get an exchange rate kicker on their equity returns.

It should also be pointed out that investing directly into less developed markets overseas also carries political and regulatory risk. You can never be sure how politicians or other pressure groups are going to change the terms under which companies are allowed to operate in less developed economies.

Tax considerations for overseas equities

While UK share purchases attract stamp duty of 0.5% of the transaction cost, most overseas equities do not. France has introduced a transaction tax, and with governments around the world looking for new ways to raise cash, there is no guarantee others won't follow suit. It is best to check online what the rules are in the country you are planning to invest in before making too many trades, as these dealing costs will hit your returns.

Before investing in US equities you should make sure your investment platform gets you to fill in a W-8BEN form, which is a Certificate of Foreign Status of Beneficial Owner for United States Tax Withholding. This basically allows you to pay less withholding tax on income from shares in these countries. A similar reduction in withholding tax is available for Canadian shares by completing their equivalent – an NR301 form.

Investing beyond the world's established economies into emerging and developing economies should be approached with the same caution as buying AIM-listed stocks, although doing so is relatively straightforward through your investment platform.

In practice, many DIY investors seeking to access overseas markets do so by investing in collective funds, such as unit trusts, OEICs, ETFs and investment trusts.

Who's who in the share trading process – stockbrokers, market makers and nominees

Understanding how the stock market actually works is essential if you are going to buy and sell shares with any regularity. Trading blue-chip shares is not problematic, but the smaller the company you want, or the larger the volume you are looking to buy, the greater the risk you can find your own actions pushing up the price. That is why it is important to understand the mechanics of the stock market.

The key players are investment platforms or stockbrokers, retail service providers (formerly called market makers), nominees and you, the share-buying customers.

Everyone has heard of a stockbroker. Back in the 1960s and 1970s the image of the bowler-hatted gent on the 07.23 into London Bridge from Tunbridge Wells wasn't that far from the truth. Before the rise of the internet, if you wanted to buy or sell shares, bonds or other securities you had to go through a stockbroker, who would arrange your deals over the phone.

These old-style stockbrokers have been largely replaced by investment platforms that, while still being stockbrokers, offer fast, cheap and easy-to-use web-based services giving you access to markets around the world. If you want an old-style stockbroker to do everything for you, there are still some around. But it will cost you.

Less well known than stockbrokers are retail service providers, yet they are equally vital to the functioning of the stock market. As their more traditional name of market maker suggests, these people are the ones who actually make the market. Think of them as a warehouse full of shares. They are standalone speculators that make the link between buyers and sellers. They play a key role in establishing the price you ultimately pay for your shares or the amount you receive when you sell them, but perhaps of equal importance is the liquidity they provide.

A nominee is the name for the company that is the legal owner of your investments and this company is typically owned by your investment platform or stockbroker. It will be a dormant company and will do nothing other than hold shares. In the event of your investment platform or stockbroker going bust, your investments are segregated and cannot be used by the liquidator or administrator to pay off your investment platform's debts.

Price

The price of something is only what someone else will pay for it. This is as true for shares as for anything else. It is worth remembering that if you see a company tipped in a Sunday newspaper for £1.00, you can be sure the market maker will have read the same article, so you may find the price has gone up to £1.05 by the time you try to buy it. Prices are all about supply and demand, and if there is no demand, the price will fall.

Investment platforms' systems usually plug into around 30 different market makers and, when you want to buy a share, offer you the one quoting the best price. When you are buying a share online, the price quoted will be held for up to 15 seconds. If you accept the price within that period, the deal is completed. If not, you have to refresh the process and start again, by which time the price may have gone up or down.

It would be a bit of a coincidence if every time someone wanted to sell some shares there was someone else wanting to buy exactly the same amount of stock. The reason there is always a price quoted for pretty much every share on every stock market in the world is because market makers are prepared to buy or sell those shares and store them in their warehouse.

The spread

The spread is more precisely the difference between the best sell price offered by the most competitive market maker and the best buy price. It is also referred to as the *bid-offer spread*.

When it comes to selling stocks in larger companies, the likelihood is the market maker will be able to offload the shares they have bought without much problem and the spread is often no more than 0.5%.

But for smaller companies, you can find the spread can exceed 2% of the share price. This is because these shares are less liquid, meaning the market maker is less confident of being able to sell them on.

Liquidity issues and exchange market size (EMS)

For very small companies, such as those listed on AIM, you can find that there is little or no market in these shares. Your investment platform may find it only receives quotes from two or three market makers interested in the stock.

Try to buy or sell a big stake in a small company online and that handful of market makers will raise or drop their price to flush out interest in moving the stock on. In this situation, rather than dealing online, you will need to phone up your investment platform and they will need to call the market makers to place the deal.

Understanding how much of a market there will be is as important when you come to sell shares as when buying them. You can check how much liquidity there is in the market by checking the stock's exchange market size (EMS). The EMS for every company traded in the UK is available on the London Stock Exchange website, in the 'Stocks' section.

The number given is the number of shares you can safely trade without the spread widening significantly. You can normally trade three times the EMS figure, although if the market goes into freefall, the market makers can turn you away and only offer you quotes at the EMS level. This can cause a problem if you build up a holding in a particular company that far exceeds the EMS level, and then need to sell them all quickly. If this happens, you can end up having to sell at a much lower price.

On the morning after the Brexit vote, the market makers were like rabbits in headlights, not knowing which way the market was going to move nor how significant any move may be. Their reaction was to reduce the market size you could trade down to virtually zero for even the most liquid stocks, meaning that the market ground to a halt for nearly two hours.

Settlement period

The settlement period is the time from the point the trade is made to the time the payment must be made to the selling party. The standard settlement period for shares is three days. This is sometimes described as T+3, T being the trading day.

For the DIY investor this has little relevance – you cannot actually buy the share unless there are sufficient funds lodged in your trading account with your investment platform. It is the investment platform who has three days to hand over the money. If you have sold shares, your investment platform will notionally credit your account with the proceeds of a sale immediately and you can use these funds to buy another investment. However, you won't be able to withdraw your funds until your investment platform has received the hard cash, which should be available for withdrawal by you on the fourth working day after sale.

Stop loss and limit orders

Stop loss and limit orders are some of the most useful tools for the DIY share investor, allowing you to get in or out of the market at predetermined levels. They are automated instructions to buy or sell shares in the event they reach a particular price. You can use them to make sure you do not suffer heavy losses or to bank gains, making them a useful way of instilling discipline into your investment process. They also liberate you from having to stare at a screen all day.

All modern investment platforms' systems are capable of setting up stop losses and limit orders on your behalf through a simple online process.

Stop loss

Also known as a stop order, a stop loss is an order to sell a stock if and when the bid or sell price falls to or below a predetermined price. The stop loss is a way to protect yourself from incurring heavy losses if a share price goes into freefall.

There is plenty of research showing that successful investing is more about doing less badly on the downside than punching the lights out on the way up. Setting stop losses is a sensible way to insure yourself against taking a complete hammering on a stock, because when a stock starts diving it does not always come back up.

A trailing stop loss is a stop loss that rises in the event that the share it is linked to rises. So if you set a 15p trailing stop loss on a stock you buy for 100p, your shares are sold if the price falls to 85p. But if the share price rises to 150p, your trailing stop loss rises with it and is fixed at 135p.

Buy limit

A buy limit is an instruction to buy a stock if the offer price drops to or below a predetermined price. This allows you to buy a stock if it hits a price you are willing to pay for it, without you having to keep watching the markets to see if it gets there.

Sell limit

A sell limit is an order to sell a stock if the bid price reaches or exceeds a price set by you in advance. You can use sell limits to bank gains in the event that shares hit what you think is a good price. Without setting a sell limit you could find yourself missing out on a profit if a share price spikes but then falls back again by the time you next check into your account to see how it is doing.

Where to set stop losses

The economic uncertainty of recent years has seen extreme volatility become a normal part of investing. With markets falling and then bouncing back on a regular basis, setting stop losses too tightly can see you simply getting out of the market at the bottom, only to see it rise up again the following day. This will lose you money.

Some shares will be more volatile than others – you can check the historic range of prices of shares through any number of online data sources. So for steady mature companies you may want to set a stop loss at a fall of somewhere around 10% or 15% of the share price, whereas you may want to go a little higher for more volatile companies.

Problems with stop losses and limit orders

Fast-falling shares, particularly those with poor liquidity, can sometimes fall past your stop loss limit before the investment platform has time to sell it. For example, if your stop loss is for 150p and the share price falls from 155p to 145p without actually hitting 150p, your shares will be sold at 145p – a lower price than you specified.

Most brokers allow you to set a two-stage stop loss order to mitigate this risk, so the order will have a trigger price that, as the names suggests, will trigger the system to try and execute the stop loss because the price has fallen below the limit you set, but there will also be a bottom price, the level that you are not prepared to sell below. So, if the share price falls dramatically, possibly on news but equally possibly on rumour, then you would not be sold out unnecessarily.

Due to fast-moving markets you need to be aware that while investment platforms will try to undertake your deal, this isn't always possible – so be careful.

Research

The internet is awash with information about the tens of thousands of companies trading on the world's stock exchanges. There is so much information out there that making sense of it all can be a challenge.

But if you are going to invest in a company and you want to satisfy yourself that it is fundamentally sound, the internet gives you the tools to do it. Company reports, sector research, financial news alerts, share tips and much more are all out there if you have the time and inclination to read them.

Remember that any tips posted on bulletin boards or in the media will already be out of date by the time you come to read them. And be alert to the fact that people promising the world on some website or social media channel are probably trying to pump up the share price of a stock they hold or dump the price of one they don't in the hope of getting in at a lower price. These anonymous posters are becoming more common on the various online bulletin boards and social media channels and are often referred to as *rampers* and *de-rampers*.

The phrase DYOR or *do your own research* is widely used by genuine posters on the bulletin boards but often ignored by newcomers to the market: it's an important discipline for the DIY investor to follow.

One source of data that you will receive at the same time as everyone else in the market is the Regulatory News Service (RNS) updates, which are formal company announcements to the market. Your investment platform should have a facility allowing you to sign up for RNS alerts by email or text. One of the most popular websites for viewing RNS statements is www.investegate.co.uk which is free to use if you are a private investor.

One way to get individual company investment ideas is to look at the holdings of top fund managers in a particular sector. Unit trusts all publish their top holdings and there is nothing to stop you piggybacking on the research of well-resourced professional fund management houses by simply buying what they hold.

If you want to keep a general eye on markets, *Shares* magazine publishes a comprehensive summary of all the key share price movements each morning, as well as news stories throughout the day. These can be read for free at www.sharesmagazine.co.uk, where you can also access a wide range of investing tools and services.

Level 2 market data

If you are serious about trading on a regular basis, you will need access to more information than is freely available on the internet. By paying for what is known as Level 2 information, you gain access to comprehensive and in-depth data on trading activity. Level 2 information is provided by some investment platforms, usually for a fixed subscription fee, or you can access it direct from information providers such as ADVFN, the London Stock Exchange and ShareScope.

Accessing Level 2 data will give you a greater picture of the factors and trends underlying share price movements at exactly the same time as professional dealers. Charges can range between £50 and £200 a quarter, depending on the amount of data you want to source.

Level 2 market data gives information on:

- orders awaiting execution on the buy and sell side of the order book
- analysis of movements in prices
- factors that can help identify automated trading patterns.

Financial ratios

Financial ratios are a way of measuring the value and profitability of companies. Understanding them is important if you are planning to actively trade equities on a regular basis. Financial ratios cover liquidity (the availability of cash to pay debt or dividends), activity (converting non-cash assets into cash), debt (the company's ability to pay down their debts) and profitability.

You will see many financial ratios published in a company's accounts, and there is lots more information available online. Research and analysis of companies is a massive subject and there are many great books out there that can tell you how to do it, so I will not go into it in a detailed way here.

I will, however, mention two of the most important ones – the P/E ratio and the dividend yield ratio.

P/E ratio

The price-to-earnings ratio, or P/E ratio, is the price of the share divided by the earnings per share. This is one of the most widely used valuations of companies.

P/E ratios are often used to compare companies within an industry, sector or market. If similar businesses have very different P/E ratios then those companies with lower ones may be perceived as being undervalued, or their growth prospects may not be as good as the company with the higher ratio.

A thumbnail guide to P/E ratios

- *Negative*: A company making a loss has an undefined P/E ratio.

- *P/E 0–10*: The company may be undervalued or its business may be in decline.

- *P/E 10–18*: Considered fair value in historical terms for companies in mature markets.

- *P/E 18–25*: Could be a growth stock with good prospects, or could be overvalued.

- *P/E 25+*: As with many emerging market stocks, high P/E ratios indicate a strong belief in the market that a company will deliver high returns in the future.

Dividends

Dividends are payments companies make to their shareholders to pass on some of their profits. They are the investor's reward for risking their capital in the company. Not all of the profits a company makes are paid as dividends, with some cash usually being held back to reinvest in the business.

Shares yielding high dividends have been favourites of both income and growth investors in recent years as cash-rich companies have made record payouts to shareholders.

If it is income you are after, high-yielding blue-chip stocks will usually give you more than cash on deposit, and can act as a hedge – or protection – against inflation as share prices generally go up with inflation.

But dividends are also valuable for growth-seekers. By reinvesting your dividends in the company you can potentially get the compounded effect of both the income from the shares and any increase in share price.

How dividends are paid

The dividend is a fixed amount per share, typically paid twice a year but sometimes quarterly. Some companies also pay one-off dividends which are called special dividends.

Any dividends you receive from your investments will be paid into your cash account with your investment platform. You can leave it in there to invest in other assets at a later date, set up an instruction for it to be automatically reinvested, or have it paid into your nominated bank or building society account.

Dividend payments are treated as a form of income and so they are subject to income tax if your investments are held outside of an ISA or SIPP. As we have covered previously, the first £2,000 (2021/22) of dividend income each year is tax-free. Above this allowance, basic-rate taxpayers pay tax at 7.5%, higher rate taxpayers at 32.5% and additional rate taxpayers at 38.1%.

In case you wondered what happens to a share price around dividend payment time, I will explain. A company's dividend is not automatically paid to the person that owns the shares on dividend pay day.

Instead, each company has an ex-dividend date, often several weeks before the dividend is paid. If you buy shares on or after the ex-dividend date, you won't receive the forthcoming dividend payment. The person who owned the stock when it went ex-dividend gets that chunk of change. You will see the share price drop by the value of the dividend as it goes ex-dividend.

You can often tell which stocks are trading ex-dividend because they'll have a special designation in stock listings, such as an 'xd' next to their name.

A *scrip* dividend is a dividend paid out in the form of extra shares in the company.

Understanding dividends – dividend yield ratio

A share's dividend yield, also known as its dividend-price ratio is, technically speaking, the company's total annual dividend payments divided by its market capitalisation.

It can more simply be calculated by dividing the dividend per share by the price of the share, multiplied by 100. So if a share costs 200p and it pays an 8p dividend, it has a 4% dividend yield.

An historic dividend yield is calculated using dividends that have been paid, whereas a forward dividend yield is calculated using the market's estimates of future dividends. In both cases the current price is used.

As explained above, preference shares pay predetermined dividends. All other dividends are payable at the discretion of the company's board and are therefore not guaranteed. If they think they have not got enough cash in the bank to pay them, dividends can be reduced or suspended altogether.

The backward-looking nature of dividend yields – a cautionary tale

It is worth stressing that dividend yields are normally backward-looking statistics, and are as much a function of the share price as of the amount that will be paid in future.

For example, at the end of 2007, banking group Lloyds had been paying a dividend of around 7.4% and its share price was in the 450p bracket. The week before Lehman Brothers collapsed in 2008, its share price had fallen to 289p and, on the basis of the historic dividend paid, divided by its now shrunken share price, its dividend yield had soared well into double figures.

An income-seeking investor looking solely at the company's dividend yield would have thought Lloyds a great bet. Unfortunately, the following Monday Lehman collapsed and within four months Lloyds shares tanked to almost a tenth of their 2007 value, and Lloyds stopped paying dividends until 2015.

Payout ratio

Arguably a more accurate way of assessing a company's dividend is its payout ratio. This is calculated by dividing the dividend by the earnings per share. If the payout ratio is greater than 1, the company is paying out more in dividends than it is earning. Unlike dividend yield, a company's payout ratio is not, therefore, affected by market sentiment towards the company's share price.

A small word of warning: earnings per share can be manipulated by clever accounting, so a company can occasionally seem like it is making enough money to comfortably pay dividends when it is not. In reality, it is cash that funds the dividends, so you need to study the cash flow of a company to accurately assess whether it has enough money to reward shareholders with dividends, or whether it is actually dipping into its savings or using debt to fund the payment (which is ultimately unsustainable).

Choosing good dividend-paying stocks

UK blue-chips have historically been among the best dividend payers in the world. The average yield on the FTSE 100 stood at around 3.3% in March 2021, compared to 2% for the S&P 500.

Within the FTSE 100 there are lots of mature companies that have paid dividends way in excess of returns for cash on deposit. In 2019 banking groups Lloyds and HSBC both paid a dividend of 6%.

Demand for income has also pushed up the price of high-dividend-yielding companies, giving investors in them a double boost.

Financial data provider ShareScope is a good source of information on the best dividend-paying companies in the UK via its SharePad online service.

Of course there are risks in holding equities – neither share price gains nor dividends are guaranteed. But they do offer some protection against inflation – unlike cash on deposit – as equities tend to rise when the prices of goods and services rise. And by buying a basket of high-income equities you can spread the risk of one of them going bad.

People who buy and hold equities long term are often investment platforms' least profitable customers. That is why some investment platforms charge a custody fee or a quarterly inactivity fee for investors who are not actively trading. If you want to buy and hold income shares, make sure you use an investment platform that is not going to penalise you for doing so.

Corporate actions – rights issues, open offers and takeovers

Corporate actions are changes to the structure of a company that affect the shares you hold. The key corporate actions for DIY investors are takeovers, rights issues and consolidations, although there are less of these than there were a decade ago. Some require shareholder votes, while others are determined by management.

Rights issues

A rights issue is a way for a company to raise more cash by issuing more shares. Under a rights issue the company offers existing shareholders the right to buy the new shares before anyone else. The price offered, known as the *call cost*, is usually lower than the current market price and shareholders are all offered new shares at the same ratio – for example, you can buy one new share for every two shares you already hold.

You can either take up a rights issue, allow it to lapse (which means the company will sell the *nil paid rights* and pay you the proceeds) or sell the *nil paid rights* in the market. This is not a likely course of action, and is only worthwhile if you have a large position.

Rights issues are commission-free and also free of stamp duty.

Companies have rights issues for a number of reasons – it could be they need to refinance their business or want to invest in new markets, or they may want cash to fund an acquisition of another company. Deciding whether to accept a rights issue will involve considering what you think of the management's reasoning behind the rights issue. You should be able to get a feel for what the experts think through commentary in the media.

Any shares not taken up by shareholders are then offered to the market or taken by the underwriter of the rights issue.

Open offer

An open offer is a cash-raising exercise like a rights issue, except the shareholder does not have the opportunity to sell the right to buy the shares to a third-party. It is a take it or leave it offer.

Another difference is that although the ratio of shares you are offered guarantees you a minimum number of shares, you can often apply for more. This is called an excess application.

Takeover

If a company you hold becomes the target of a takeover it is usually good news for its share price. The takeover has to be approved by a proportion of the shareholders, although if the bidding company acquires 90% of the shares of the target company then it can force the acquisition of the remaining target company's shares.

The bidding company usually pays for the shares in either cash or shares in itself. Accepting a share offer does not crystallise gains for capital gains tax purposes. When you sell or dispose of your new shares they are treated as if you bought them at the same time and cost as your original shares.

Some bidding companies offer loan notes instead of cash. This, too, can help an individual defer a capital gains tax liability, while giving them the security of fixing a price for offloading their shares.

Shareholder perks

Being a part-owner of a company by virtue of holding its shares can, in some cases, bring with it special shareholder perks which are tax-free. Some companies require you to have a set amount of shares before you get access to the perks. Some companies will not offer shareholder perks if the shares are held in nominee, and some investment platforms take the view that the administration of dealing with these perks is too much trouble. I would urge you not to buy a share just for the perks and if they are important to you, check out whether your chosen investment platform will pass them on to you.

Either way, shareholder perks are not as generous as they were years ago, and fewer and fewer companies are offering them.

Shareholder perks – some of the best

- *Fuller, Smith & Turner* – 15% discount on food and drinks in any of its managed pubs and hotels, plus 15% off certain rates in its hotels.

- *InterContinental Hotels* – discounted rates at its hotels.

- *BT* – discounted phones, tablets and Wi-Fi equipment.

- *Mulberry Group* – 20% off up to £5,000 of merchandise a year.

Tax considerations for equities

Hopefully you are getting the drift of tax considerations, as equities are taxed similarly to funds.

Returns from equities come in two ways – dividends and growth in share price.

Dividends are treated as income and therefore your dividend income is added to your other income on your tax return and you pay tax on it at your marginal rate.

Growth in the value of your shares is subject to capital gains tax at the time you sell them, if the increase in value exceeds your annual allowance.

For equities held within an ISA or a SIPP, you do not need to think about tax when deciding to go for equities that will give you growth or income. But for any equities outside a tax-advantaged wrapper, it can make sense to go for whichever will give you the lowest tax bill – though saving tax should not be the sole motivation for making an investment.

The risks of equities

Equities are at the riskier end of the investment spectrum and should be handled with care. Invest in them only if you fully understand them. And that means understanding that you may not get all, or indeed any, of your money back if the company performs badly. Share prices may fall, dividends may be reduced or stopped altogether; companies may even go bust, leaving investors completely out of pocket.

It would be foolish to suggest that buying and selling equities like a day trader is going to make you a million. But, despite their risks, a well-diversified portfolio of shares is likely, in the long term, to generate higher returns than you would get from most other asset classes.

Top websites

- www.advfn.com
- www.investorschronicle.co.uk
- www.londonstockexchange.com
- www.sharesmagazine.co.uk

12

CORPORATE BONDS AND GILTS

Less risky than equities but usually returning more than cash held in a bank or building society, bonds aim to give a steady income through good times and bad. Understanding bonds is all about understanding risk, and, as with investments across the board, the more risk you are prepared to take, the greater the returns you can hope to get.

Before the credit crunch and the Eurozone crisis that followed it, many people hadn't a clue about corporate or government bonds. Today we are all too familiar with the idea that nations and other organisations see their borrowing costs go up if the bond markets don't trust in their ability to pay their debts.

Bonds are issued by governments and companies to raise capital to pay for high-cost projects, from wars to railways to housing projects, and, in the case of many debt-ridden nations these days, to pay the interest on existing liabilities. They are promises to pay an annual sum, the *coupon*, for a fixed term, in return for the bondholder lending the issuing organisation a lump sum of money, known as the *principal*. The principal is also refunded to the bondholder at the maturity date.

By investing in a bond you effectively become a lender to the country, company or other organisation issuing it. Once you have handed over your cash to the bond issuer you have nothing other than a piece of paper containing a promise to pay you back. If that bond issuer then goes bust you are out of pocket. So to reward you for taking on the risk of their bonds, issuers pay you an annual or six-monthly coupon – the more likely a borrowing company or country is to go bust, the higher the coupon they pay.

Bonds issued by the UK government are called *gilts*, short for *gilt-edged security*, which is precisely what Bank of England bonds were until the last century. The bonds issued by the Bank of England were large pieces of paper with gold-leaf edges that were divided into sections. Each section was a coupon that reflected a payment due to the holder, and would be ripped off and given back to the issuer upon receipt of the sum due. When all of the coupons had been ripped off, the bond expired and the principal sum was repaid.

While there are no gold-leaf-edged parchments any more, the principle behind today's bonds is exactly the same.

Gilts are arguably among the safest investments in the world and the returns they offer are low on account of this. In March 2021, the return on ten-year gilts stood at 0.76% per year. To reflect its rather higher risk profile, anyone prepared to invest in ten-year bonds issued by the Indian government at that time earned a return of 6.2% per year.

Corporate bonds range from the very secure, offered by cash-rich blue-chip companies, right up the risk scale to the very insecure, known as *junk bonds*, offered by struggling companies facing financial headwinds, or early-stage companies whose prospects are unclear.

Bonds had, until the turn of the century, traditionally been accessed through stockbrokers, or through unit trusts and OEICs investing in baskets of them. But the advent of online investment platforms has brought them to a wider audience of investors who are looking to beat miserable cash-on-deposit rates by taking on a little extra risk.

For years, investors wanting to take a DIY approach to the bond market were only really able to do so if they had very large portfolios. That was because the minimum threshold for investing in bonds was between £10,000 and £50,000. You could access bonds for less than this in the past, but not as a retail investor.

But over the past few decades we have seen a trend, albeit a slow one, of companies offering retail bonds direct to consumers, knowing they can beat the cash rates on deposit and still raise funds more cheaply than going to a bank for a loan.

This market took a step forward when the London Stock Exchange launched its Order Book for Retail Bonds (ORB) in 2010. This created a market for the trading of bonds aimed at retail investors wanting to invest far smaller sums. Since then, a few household-name companies, from National Grid to Tesco, have offered bonds to retail investors, with a minimum investment threshold of just £1,000.

ORB has created a more efficient market for the DIY investor, with far tighter bid/offer spreads on the buying and selling of corporate bonds. However, the volume of new bonds being issued remains only a fraction of the number of companies joining the stock market. As such, retail bonds remain a niche proposition for most investors.

The history of corporate bonds and gilts

People have been using bonds to raise money for literally thousands of years. Archaeologists tell us the oldest surety bond that has ever been found dates back to 2400BC and is from Mesopotamia (modern-day Iraq). It is a piece of stone with carved letters guaranteeing the payment of grain.

Governments have been issuing bonds to pay for wars for centuries. In fact, the ability of nations and political groups to raise money for wars through bonds has been one of the key driving forces of the history of the world. These have usually been big-ticket bonds issued to institutions and wealthy families, but cash-strapped countries have also regularly appealed to the nationalist fervour of their populations to issue war bonds available to the man or woman in the street.

Rothschild, bonds and the Battle of Waterloo

Nathan Mayer Rothschild was one of the most celebrated bond dealers history has ever known. Not only did he help defeat Napoleon by bankrolling Wellington's troops, he also knew a thing or two about how to play the bond markets.

Fully understanding the value of up-to-date information on financial markets, Rothschild placed an agent near the Battle of Waterloo, knowing a victory for Napoleon would be a terrible blow to the British economy that would wipe millions off the value of his massive holding of British government bonds.

Rothschild's agent arrived in London a day before Wellington's courier and delivered the momentous news to his boss. The story goes that Rothschild went to the stock exchange and stood hanging his head, selling large amounts of British government bonds. Falling for his bluff, all the other traders started selling their bonds too and prices fell to the floor. Rothschild's agents duly hoovered them up at rock-bottom prices, only to see their value bounce back up again when the actual result of the battle came through.

Corporate bonds have been in existence for almost as long as there have been companies, with the East India Company and the Dutch East India Company both issuing bonds early in the 17th century.

The first decades of the 20th century saw an increase in the issue of corporate bonds. These early issues were mainly investment-grade bonds, with appetite for junk bonds verging on the non-existent.

The modern market in non-investment-grade, or high-yield bonds, really took off after the financial crisis of the 1970s. Falling asset prices led banks to lend only to those companies with a strong credit rating.

The 1980s saw high-yield bonds delivering excellent returns without the increased levels of defaults their yields suggested, attracting increasing numbers of investors to the asset class. In the USA, yields through the 1980s averaged 14.5%, while default rates averaged just 2.2%.

Yes, there have been collapses as long as there have been companies issuing them, but corporate bonds have continued to deliver steady returns more often than not. On rare occasions, canny investors (such as Rothschild two centuries ago) have been able to make money out of overreactions to negative sentiment about corporations. But most investors prefer it when bonds do what they are supposed to, which is generate boring but reliable returns, year in, year out.

That said, be in no doubt that companies can and will go bust. Most will come good, but there is a risk that if people come to perceive these bonds as akin to cash on deposit with a bank, one day someone, or more accurately several thousand investors, are going to wake up to a nasty surprise.

The financial crisis, the Eurozone and corporate bonds

Back at the height of the credit crunch in 2008, investors were staring into the abyss and fearing the worst. Fear of corporate collapse meant bond prices fell off a cliff, meaning the income you got for buying them soared. Don't get me wrong, the doom and gloom at the time was very real – who would have thought that Lehman Brothers, Bear Stearns and many more household-name companies at home and abroad would be consigned to history? But bond managers knew that valuations had fallen far further than the fundamentals justified.

Back in October 2008 corporate bond prices had fallen so far that, for anyone holding a basket of stocks, at least a third of investment-grade issuers would have had to go bust over the next five years before investing in government bonds would have delivered a better return. In other words, one-in-three major companies in the UK would need to be wiped out in a financial collapse greater than the Wall Street Crash of 1929.

The fear that stalked investors back in 2008 meant that the Investment Management Association sterling high-yield bond sector, which tracks riskier bonds, saw an average fall of 25% in 2008. But when the world didn't completely melt down, the rebound in 2009 was 48%.

Concerns over corporate bond defaults became much more muted as corporate Britain accumulated stockpiles of cash having pulled in its horns and trimmed its operating expenses. Instead, the focus switched to sovereign debt – the bonds issued by nation states.

The financial crisis suddenly woke up the markets to the fact that some countries in southern Europe might actually go bust and not repay the loans they had taken from the world's banks. The so-called PIIGS – Portugal, Ireland, Italy, Greece and Spain – found themselves on the critical list, with even France seeing its cost of borrowing soar as Germany persisted in its refusal to share these other countries' liabilities by issuing Eurobonds.

Outside the Eurozone, meanwhile, the UK's budget-trimming measures and its ability to print money and devalue its currency earned it safe-haven status around the world. With foreign cash rushing from the continent into gilts, their prices have soared, pushing gilt yields down to historic lows, leaving them struggling to beat inflation, and punishing annuity rates and savers' interest rates.

For those unfamiliar with how prices and yields work on bond and gilts, the yield will fall as its price rises, and vice versa.

Textbooks can be wrong. Government and corporate bonds are meant to be steady, solid investments. And it is true that if you hold a bond until maturity, you know exactly what return you will get – provided the issuer remains solvent.

But it is worth bearing in mind that, not just in the extraordinary circumstances we have seen in the past decade, bonds can default.

Bond terminology

You should be able to access market data on bonds through your investment platform, or from a number of other sources across the industry (see below). It is important to understand what the various pieces of jargon from the world of bonds actually mean, and how they all piece together.

Conventional gilts

These are the simplest form of gilts. They pay a fixed coupon, usually twice a year, and mature on a fixed date. They can last for a few months or several decades. Some have *calls* that allow the government to pay them off early. Always check the small print of what you are buying before completing your purchase. The gilts most commonly used by individuals are those with between two and ten years left to run.

Index-linked gilts

Like index-linked bonds, these pay a coupon that is indexed to the Retail Price Index (RPI). The principal is also indexed in a similar way. They offer the investor a protection against inflation.

Maturity date

As it sounds – the maturity date is the date the bond expires and the principal is repaid to the bondholder. The date or year of maturity is usually contained in the name of the bond, for example 5% Treasury Gilt 2025 or Tesco plc 6% 2029.

Gilts are categorised in relation to their maturity, with short defined as 0–7 years, medium as 7–15 years and long anything 15 years or more.

Ultra short gilts have a maturity of less than three years, while those issued since 2005 with a maturity of 50 years are *ultra long*.

Corporate bonds don't have a formal short, medium and long naming convention, but a rule of thumb is that short is anything between 0 and 5 years, medium is 5 to 12 years, and long is anything over 12 years.

Coupon

This is the rate of interest the bond agreed to pay at the outset. The coupon rate will normally also be in the name of the bond.

Issue date

The date the bond was first issued.

Income yield

The income yield, also known as the current yield or running yield, is the percentage return the bond is delivering at a particular point in time. Put another way, it is the annual coupon divided by the price, expressed as a percentage. It therefore only reflects the annual interest payment and the price paid.

So, a bond with a face value of £100 that pays out £5 has an income yield of 5%. If the price of the bond goes down, to say £50, the income yield goes up to 10%.

Par value and price

When bonds are issued, they are at *par value*, which means face value. If any of the risk factors that influence bond values reduce their value below this level, they are described as *below par*, while if their value rises above the par value they are said to be *above par*.

The issue price for bonds issued on the London Stock Exchange is 100, which is par value. The figure shown as *price* on its website reflects the percentage of par at which the bond is currently trading. So if its price is shown as 90, that means the price of the bond has fallen by 10% since the issue date.

Gross redemption yield

The gross redemption yield, also known as the yield to maturity, is arguably the most important yield for investors. It is a measure that reflects the overall rate of return of the bond. It is the effective rate of return the investor will get if they buy a bond and hold it until it matures. It is a useful figure because it gives you a clear view of the return you are getting compared to other more secure interest rates available on the market.

The figure not only assumes all coupons will be paid and the principal redeemed, but also that you will be able to reinvest the coupon payments and earn the same return, which may not in fact be possible. It also reflects the repayment of the principal at the end of the term. So if you have bought a bond at less than par, your gross redemption yield will include the capital gain you will make.

You should note that the gross redemption yield makes no allowance for tax.

The risks of bonds and how these affect their value

A company's bonds are less risky than its equities because in the event the entity goes bust, bondholders rank higher in priority when it comes to paying out what remains of the company's assets than shareholders.

But that does not mean they do not carry any risk. The key risk to a bond is that the company goes bust and is unable to pay. If that happens, the company is wound up and once other creditors have been paid out, bondholders may or may not get a certain number of pennies in the pound of their investment back, although it could take years.

If you hold the bond until redemption, and the issuer remains solvent, then you will get precisely the return you are expecting – namely the coupons for the remainder of the term of the bond, plus the return of the principal.

If you sell the bond before maturity, however, then there are other risk factors that can make the value of the bond you hold fluctuate up or down. These are the length of time until redemption, changes to the company's fundamental strength or lack of it, and the interest rate environment. The manner and extent to which these factors impact your bond-holding's value will also depend on whether you purchased it at par, above par or below par. Another less tangible risk to holding bonds is inflation, which in the case of government bonds can be mitigated by investing in index-linked bonds.

Bonds approaching maturity

As the bond's redemption date approaches, the greater certainty you will have that the issuer is going to be able to pay back the principal. This means its value will, all other things being equal, approach par.

Issuer credit risk

The company or government that issued the bond may have been in rude financial health when you took out the bond, but since then it may have run into financial difficulties. Bond markets ultimately match the payoff between the return being offered by the bond against the risk of the issuer defaulting.

So if analysts think your bond-issuer's prospects have declined since you bought it, it will negatively affect the bond's value. If you have taken a bet on a junk bond with a risky company that has subsequently turned a corner towards financial strength, and the ratings agencies have upgraded its credit rating, the value of your bond will go up.

If you hold the bond to maturity and the issuer does not go bust, then the changes in the value of the bond will not affect you as you will have received precisely the coupons and maturity proceeds you envisaged when you invested.

The effect of interest rates

Changes to the market's expectations of future interest rates have a big impact on the value of bonds. At its most simple level, if something happens to lead the market to expect interest rates to rise then the value of a bond will fall. The longer a bond has to maturity, the more sensitive its price is likely to be to a change in interest-rate expectations.

These two statements oversimplify what is a complex interaction between market expectations of interest rates and the price of a bond, which is also influenced by inflation, wider views of the economy and many other factors.

Inflation-linked bonds

High inflation erodes the value of fixed-income bonds, which refers to most conventional gilt and corporate bonds.

If you are concerned about inflation you can opt for bonds that increase their payout in line with inflation. National Grid issued the first inflation-linked corporate bond ever to be made available to retail investors in 2011, paying 1.25% above the Retail Price Index. Since then, Tesco has launched one paying 1% above RPI.

Index-linked gilts have been around for years – since 1981 to be precise – when the very first one was issued by the-then chancellor, Geoffrey Howe.

No compensation

Corporate bonds must be distinguished from the sorts of bonds issued by banks and building societies. Bonds issued by financial organisations of this sort, often described as *fixed-rate bonds*, benefit from the protection of the Financial Services Compensation Scheme, which guarantees to pay up to £85,000 of losses incurred in the event that a bank or building society bond issuer goes bust.

Corporate bonds and gilts, on the other hand, do not benefit from Financial Services Compensation Scheme protection if the issuer goes bust.

You need to read the small print to make sure you fully understand which type of bond you are investing in. The line between the two types of bond can become blurred when a financial services organisation issues a retail corporate bond.

For example, Tesco Bank has issued a number of corporate bonds that do not come with Financial Services Compensation Scheme protection. But it also offers a range of fixed-rate savings accounts that might also be described as bonds, which do come with investor protection.

People often mistakenly believe that because bond investments are promoted as being safer than equity investments, they carry some form of capital protection. They don't, unless you hold them to maturity and of course the company has sufficient funds to repay the bond.

How bonds are risk-rated

There are several ratings agencies that assess bond issuers' ability to pay back their debts. Ratings agencies have many different gradations of risk, but corporate bonds are generally divided into two clearly defined sectors – investment-grade and high-yield or junk bonds.

As a DIY investor, if you are going to make direct investments into bonds, you should only touch investment-grade ones, unless you really know what you are doing. If you want to access high-yield bonds, it is best to do it through a fund.

Before buying a bond you should check where the issuer stands in the league table of risk. Standard & Poor's, Moody's and other ratings agencies give free access to their ratings of thousands of companies and governments around the world, provided you register with them. Ratings for companies are provided, as well as the agency's view on the outlook for them and other research supporting this.

Investment-grade bonds

Also known as high-grade corporate bonds, investment-grade bonds are those issued by companies perceived by the ratings agencies to be the most secure. Each ratings agency has their own way of ranking companies. For Standard & Poor's, a company with a credit rating of BBB– and higher is considered investment-grade. Under Moody's ratings, companies must be Baa3 or higher to qualify as investment-grade.

These ratings apply equally to countries – the downgrade of a country's investment rating can be politically and economically damaging.

High-yield/junk bonds

Anything rated below these levels is considered a high-yield or junk bond. These bonds, as you might have guessed, pay higher yields, but the chance of them going bust is also far higher. In addition, ratings agencies can downgrade high-yield bonds further, meaning their resale value will fall.

Table 12.1: Understanding ratings agency classifications

Moody's		S&P		Fitch		
Long term	Short term	Long term	Short term	Long term	Short term	
Investment						
Aaa	P-1	AAA	A-1+	AAA	F1+	Prime
Aa1	–	AA+	–	AA+	–	High grade
Aa2	–	AA	–	AA	–	–
Aa3	–	AA-	–	AA-	–	–
A1	–	A+	A-1	A+	F1	Upper medium grade
A2	–	A	–	A	–	–
A3	P-2	A-	A-2	A-	F2	–
Baa1	–	BBB+	–	BBB+	–	Lower medium grade
Baa2	P-3	BBB	A-3	BBB	F3	–
Baa3	–	BBB-	–	BBB-	–	–
Ba1	Not prime	BB+	B	BB+	B	Non-investment grade speculative
Ba2	–	BB	–	BB	–	–
Ba3	–	BB-	–	BB-	–	–
B1	B+	–	B+	–	Highly speculative	
B2	B	–	B	–	–	
B3	B-	–	B-	–	–	

Moody's		S&P		Fitch		
Long term	Short term	Long term	Short term	Long term	Short term	
Junk						
Caa1	–	CCC+	C	CCC	C	Substantial risks
Caa2	–	CCC	–	–	–	Extremely speculative
Caa3	–	CCC-	–	–	–	Default imminent with little prospect for recovery
Ca	–	CC	–	–	–	–
–	–	C	–	–	–	–
C	–	D	/	DDD	/	In default
/	–	–	–	DD	–	–
/	–	–	–	D	–	–

Safety of gilts

In the more than 300 years since it was established, the Bank of England has never defaulted on any of its liabilities. That does not mean it is the most secure bank in the world today. Today, bond markets clearly think the German central bank offers investors more security, which is why its cost of borrowing is lower than the UK government's.

But while they might not quite beat the Bundesbank when it comes to security, gilts – bonds issued by the Bank of England – are still among the most rock-steady investments in the world. Despite the massive deficit the UK carries, it had until recently maintained its AAA rating with all the major ratings agencies. Even the mighty USA saw its rating cut by

Standard & Poor's in 2011 to AA+ over its budget concerns. France saw its S&P downgraded by the same degree at the beginning of 2012.

Ratings agencies downgraded their ratings on the UK following the EU referendum vote in June 2016. The decision for the UK to leave the EU prompted S&P to cut its rating from AAA to AA. Moody's cut the UK's credit rating outlook to negative.

The mechanics of buying, holding and selling corporate bonds and gilts

DIY investors can either buy bonds through a bond fund or hold them directly. Both ways of holding bonds can be achieved through an investment platform.

Bond and gilt funds

If you buy a bond fund, the fund manager will endeavour to buy and sell bonds as their value changes, attempting to deliver you a return from the coupon paid on the bond and also on the bonds themselves hopefully rising in value.

There are two main types of bond fund – those that simply target a part of the market, for example investment-grade or high-yield, or *strategic* bond funds that allow the fund manager to move from one type to the other as and when they feel fit.

Bond funds give you access to an expert managing bond purchases and sales on your behalf, and your risk is spread by virtue of the fact you are investing in a basket of many different bonds. But you will also pay an annual management charge for the privilege. In normal conditions, investment returns from bond funds will be modest, at best, so you need to ensure that fund management charges are not disproportionately high.

That said, in the extraordinary markets of recent years, most of the top bond managers have proved their worth and justified their annual management charges.

However, if you are passionate about cutting charges to a minimum, there is less scope to do so in the world of corporate bonds. While it is relatively easy for DIY investors to cut out the cost of the fund manager and create their own equity portfolio, this strategy is harder for corporate bonds. This is because you can't always get good liquidity in the market with small amounts of a corporate bond. Unless you have a very large amount of money to invest, this makes getting a diversified corporate bond portfolio prohibitively expensive.

If the relatively high costs proportionate to the returns on the bond fund make it unappealing then you have two alternatives. You can get exposure to the whole of your chosen part of the bond market (most likely UK investment-grade) through a low-cost bond ETF or OEIC tracker. Or you can build your own portfolio of directly held gilts and retail corporate bonds from the 140 or so that are available through the London Stock Exchange's ORB service.

If you want to invest in bonds via an ETF or tracker OEIC then there are many indices that track the UK and overseas gilt and corporate bond markets.

Buying a bond fund or ETF is done in exactly the same way as any other form of collective investment.

Buying and selling bonds

You can buy your retail corporate bond either at the time it is issued, known as the *primary market*, or second-hand in the *secondary market*. You can check what retail bonds are either available for subscription or about to come to market by keeping an eye on the 'New and recent issues on ORB' page in the bonds section of the London Stock Exchange website.

There you will find a list of the stockbrokers that are sponsoring the bond issue, as well as the prospectus and other information about the bond. Minimum investments are either £1,000 or £2,000, depending on the issuer, with increments going up in steps of £100 thereafter.

It must be noted that there were very few new bond issues between 2015 and 2020, suggesting that companies have been finding it easier to borrow money from alternative sources while interest rates have been so low in the UK.

Some but not all investment platforms have a direct link to the London Stock Exchange's ORB service. If one does, then the cost of buying existing retail corporate bonds will typically be similar to any other trade, usually around £10. There is normally no explicit charge for investing in a new issue as your investment platform will receive between 0.5% and 1% of the investment as commission.

You can buy and sell gilts through the government's Debt Management Office, but it will be easier, quicker and probably cheaper to do this through your investment platform. Dealing charges for gilts are likely to be the same as for corporate bonds.

There is no stamp duty payable on purchases of gilts or corporate bonds.

Spreads and settlement period

As for equities, there is a spread on both corporate bonds and gilts – the difference between the price at which you buy and the price at which you sell. The more liquid the bond, the lower the spread, so typically you will find that gilts have a smaller spread than corporate bonds, and the bigger the bond issue, the smaller the spread.

The settlement period for corporate bonds is the time from the point the trade is made to the time the payment must be made to the selling party. The conventional settlement period for gilts is one day, also described as T+1, with T being the trading day, although many providers nowadays settle on T+3, in line with equities. For corporate bonds the settlement period is T+3.

Research

One of the best websites for gilts is the Debt Management Office's website, www.dmo.gov.uk.

You will find a full list of all gilts in existence with the key information for each of them.

WebFinancial and Bloomberg also have good basic information on gilts including prices.

Before you buy corporate bonds you need to research the companies issuing them. You can:

- Check RNS announcements via London Stock Exchange's website to see if there have been any warnings given that would raise concerns about the company's financial position.

- Check the company's accounts to see if it is profitable and also check its interest cover. This is the ratio that shows how easily a firm will be able to meet its debt interest repayments. This is calculated by dividing earnings before interest and taxes (EBIT) by interest payments.

- Check what the bond debt is secured against, and where it stands in the priority order in the event of insolvency. This information should be available in the prospectus.

- Check the company's rating with any of the big ratings agencies. Compare the relationship between the rating and the return being offered with other similar companies to see if you are taking more risk than you need to for the return you are getting.

- If these four steps sound too complicated then stick to bond funds as the fund managers will do all the checks as part of their day job.

Tax rules and considerations

Coupon payments on bonds and gilts are taxable as income at your marginal rate.

You can hold bonds and gilts in a dealing account, ISA or a SIPP.

Income received from bonds and gilts is normally paid gross. It is also treated as interest for the purposes of the personal savings allowance described in previous chapters.

The good news is there is no capital gains tax on gilts or on qualifying corporate bonds if their value increases for whatever reason, including indexation increases to the principal for index-linked gilts. Most corporate bonds you can buy will qualify for this relief; only those with special features, such as the ability to be turned into shares at a later date, do not qualify. Capital losses on bonds cannot be used to offset other capital gains.

SIPPs and ISAs incur no tax on bond income or capital gains. If you hold bonds personally through a dealing account, you will account for any tax due via your self-assessment tax return.

There is no stamp duty when you buy bonds.

Permanent interest-bearing shares (PIBS)

Permanent interest-bearing shares (PIBS) are a special class of share issued by building societies. They pay a fixed rate of interest and can be bought and sold on the stock exchange. They have some of the characteristics of a corporate bond, in that they pay a fixed income on a regular basis, but they normally run for an indeterminate period. Some PIBS, however, have a *call date*, which gives the issuer the right to buy the PIBS back from you if it wants to.

PIBS issued by building societies that have subsequently demutualised are called perpetual sub-bonds (PSBs).

Payment of returns

Returns are normally fixed, although some building societies will issue floating rate PIBS that pay a certain percentage above a given price index. That said, the returns are fixed only up to the extent that the building society's financial strength permits them to be paid. Returns are normally paid six-monthly on predetermined dates.

The risks of PIBS

Building societies issue PIBS to raise capital because, being mutuals rather than limited companies, they do not have the power to raise capital by issuing shares. Therefore the ability of the PIBS to continue being able to pay out is dependent on the financial strength of the issuing building society.

PIBS-holders are last in priority to be paid out in the event that a building society becomes insolvent.

Unlike other building society investors, PIBS-holders do not benefit from protection of up to £85,000 from the Financial Services Compensation Scheme in the event that the society goes bust.

The resale price of PIBS can also go down or up depending on other factors in the wider economy. Back in the early 1990s, for example, when bank base rates were in double digits, PIBS paying out 12% or 13% a year were not that extraordinary. These days, with interest rates at historic lows, PIBS paying out at these levels are valuable things, which is why they trade above par.

But be careful about buying PIBS at a premium. Their value is likely to fall in the event that interest rates rise. And if your PIBS has a call date then there is always the risk that the issuing building society will buy them back at face value when that date comes around.

When PIBS go wrong

When many PIBS were launched back in the early 1990s, a number of investors assumed they were as rock solid as the building societies that issued them. Unfortunately for those who bought PIBS from Northern Rock and Bradford & Bingley, they were, as both companies subsequently had to be bailed out by the UK government

The interest rates offered were huge. Northern Rock issued PIBS paying 12.6% a year, while Bradford & Bingley issued PIBS paying 13% and 11.6%. To be fair, interest rates were considerably higher at that time than they are today, and rates like this were not uncommon. Both of these lenders' PIBS were converted to PSBs when each of the building societies demutualised.

But when the financial crisis hit and both institutions went bust, income payments ceased immediately and it was to be several more years until both sets of PIBS-holders were offered a payout of around 30p in the pound on their original investment.

PIBS-investors were also hit when Lloyds took over HBOS. Some investors were forced to sell their PIBS holdings at lower than market prices.

Then came the case of West Bromwich Building Society PIBS-holders. In 2009, the building society went through a capital restructuring that saw the terms of PIBS rewritten, wiping about 80% off their value. More recently, holders of Co-op and Manchester Building Society PIBS have been given a sharp reminder of the risks inherent in these investments.

The small print in PIBS documents does state that building societies are allowed to alter or stop income payments if making them would breach the society's capital adequacy requirements, which are the financial reserves they are legally required to hold. That is of small consolation to the PIBS-holders who feel they have been made to shoulder a disproportionate share of the burden of restoring the building society to a financially sound footing.

Buying, selling and holding PIBS

You can buy, sell and hold PIBS through your investment platform. The cost of dealing in them will typically be the same as trading any other form of share. PIBS are usually sold in blocks of 1,000, although some can only be bought in larger blocks.

Liquidity of PIBS

Liquidity of PIBS is poor because there is not a lot of trading in them. Spreads between the buy and sell price can be as wide as 10%.

Tax on PIBS

Tax on PIBS is the same as for bonds and they can be held in ISAs and SIPPs.

Top websites for research and information

- www.bloomberg.com
- www.dmo.gov.uk
- www.fitchratings.com
- www.fixedincomeinvestor.co.uk
- www.londonstockexchange.com
- www.monevator.com
- www.moodys.com
- www.standardandpoors.com
- www.thisismoney.co.uk
- www.uat.webfg.com/gilt

13

CASH

The returns you get for investing in cash may be very low indeed, but there is nothing quite like cash when it comes to security and liquidity.

You need cash for your everyday living expenses, to have as an emergency pot (more on this later) but you will also probably have times when you need to hold some of your investment assets in cash, whether for short periods or for several months. This could be while you are taking a pause to rebalance your portfolio, if you think the market does not offer good value, or if you suspect a fall in markets is looming. You might also want to opt for cash if you have a sum of money you want to put to a particular use and don't want to risk losing any of it, so buying a bigger house or paying for university fees for your children, for example. Or you could be approaching or in retirement and simply not want to expose yourself to any risk at all.

Cash is about security and access, both of which need to be understood fully when you are putting large sums on deposit, as it's not a free ride, there are payoffs to having cash.

There are different ways of holding cash, some of which offer better returns than others. There are few, if any, deals available through investment platforms that offer great returns. So, if you have large sums you want to hold on deposit for anything other than a short term, you will almost certainly do better by transferring from your investment platform to a bank or building society account.

Each of your SIPP, ISA and dealing account will normally have their own unique cash account with your investment platform. You need to think of this cash account as akin to a current account that enables you to buy and sell investments as well as receive investment income, such as dividends. These accounts pay low rates of interest and are not intended to be a long-term home for your cash.

Emergency cash pot

Every investor should have a cash pot that they can access immediately to use as a buffer in an emergency. This could be a bout of ill health or losing your job, for example. The rule of thumb for emergency cash is between three and six months' expenditure – that's to cover your essential outgoings, rather than matching six months of income. So you need to tot up how much your mortgage or rent, bills, food costs and any other essential spending costs each month to give you a ballpark figure.

Whether you save three months or six months of costs into this pot depends on your own circumstances. For example, if you're a two-income family and can afford much of your essential outgoings should one of you lose your job, you may err on the lower end of this scale, whereas if you're entirely reliant on one income you might want to have six months or even more. It's also down to your own risk appetite and whether you like to have a bigger safety blanket or not.

Best-buy savings accounts

With the Bank of England's base rate having been so low for such a long time, you really need to make sure your cash is earning the most it can. If you forget about it and leave it in the same account, it'll likely end up earning next to nothing in interest. A good rule of thumb is that if you haven't switched account in the past year or 18 months, you can probably earn more interest by moving your money elsewhere.

You can find best-buy savings account tables at comparison websites such as MoneySuperMarket, Moneyfacts and uSwitch, listed at the end of this chapter. MoneySavingExpert also has good guides that are regularly updated to the best rates for different types of accounts.

If you want to be able to get your money out straightaway, look for instant-access accounts. But be aware that this flexibility comes at a cost, as you'll usually get lower rates on these accounts. If you can live with the idea of having to wait before you get your money, go for a notice account, be it 30-day, 60-day, 90-day, 120-day or 180-day. Any longer than that and you are getting into the realm of one-year fixed-rate bonds. Notice accounts carry penalties of a certain number of days' lost interest in the event that you withdraw the cash early. The longer the notice period, the higher the interest they normally pay – but not always. If the market expects interest rates to fall in the next few months, there may be little or no difference between shorter- and longer-term deposits.

Bonus rates

Watch out for bonus rates on comparison site savings account tables. The deals with the highest interest rates usually come with a first-year bonus rate, without which they would be nowhere near table-topping. In fact, some deals with an initial bonus rate fall right down to 0.1% interest as soon as the offer period is over. If you are only investing the money for a year or less or you know that you're good at remembering to switch accounts regularly, these deals are fine – in fact they are probably the best option.

If you are putting your money away for a long time, however, only use accounts offering early period bonuses if you know you have the discipline to move your money to another provider the day the bonus deal expires. Always make a diary note for a month or so before the expiry of a bonus deal to start planning your exit strategy and find another market-leading deal.

Alternatively, you can go for a deal without a bonus rate, in the knowledge that you will get a decent enough rate over the long term – although these rates can be cut further down the line, so it's not a totally hands-free option. If you know you aren't organised enough to rearrange a new deal straightaway, these good but not market-leading rates will work out better for you in the long run.

Cash-switching tools

One way around having to remember to switch your money each time is to automate the process. A few cash-switching tools have emerged, which will make it easier to switch between accounts and saves you the hassle of all the form-filling to open a new account each time.

You sign up to the service and it offers you a range of different cash account options, depending on whether you're willing to lock your money up or not – and you're able to move your money between them when the account matures or a better rate comes up. The rates might not be quite as good as going direct with each provider, but it will probably mean you're more likely to switch accounts rather than leave your money dwindling in an account paying nothing.

This is an area that several investment platforms have moved into including AJ Bell, Hargreaves Lansdown and Interactive Investor.

Cash accounts on investment platforms

Do not expect a decent rate of return from cash you hold in the cash account of your investment platform. These accounts typically pay interest of between zero and base rate, with many paying no interest whatsoever. Some investment platforms pay you more interest the more money you have in the account, but even then it will be below the best high-street rates on offer. With bank base rates at historic lows, that means different shades of not very much for everyone.

There are alternatives to these ultra-low or non-existent interest rates offered by investment platforms, and they are covered briefly in this chapter. All but the most inactive of DIY investors will find there will inevitably be times when some cash is sitting earning little or no interest in a cash account.

The extent to which this interest rate is a relevant factor in your choice of platform will depend on how much you are holding in cash, and how often.

Cash ISA transfer

Cash ISAs are covered in Chapter 3. If you want to move your Cash ISA to take advantage of the market-leading Cash ISA rates on offer from banks and building societies, you will be able to do so.

To carry out the transfer you should be careful not to move your ISA cash into your current account first. If you do, your money could lose its tax-privileged status.

Historically, once assets were moved outside the protection of an ISA wrapper they weren't allowed to be put in again, other than through using up that year's ISA allowance. Instead you would have had to transfer the funds directly from one ISA provider to another.

Some ISAs are now more flexible – although there is a risk warning attached, as always. The government has introduced the ability for you to deposit money, withdraw some or all of it, and then put the money back in your ISA in the same tax year without affecting your annual allowance.

Let's say the annual ISA allowance is £20,000 and you deposited £12,000 into your ISA. You subsequently withdraw £5,000. Under the old rules, you would have only been allowed to put another £8,000 into your ISA in the same tax year – being the difference between what you'd already put in and the annual allowance which is currently £20,000. Under the new rules, you could deposit £13,000 – so the £8,000 plus the £5,000 which you had earlier put in the ISA and then taken out.

Here's the catch. Not every bank offers this flexibility with their ISA product. The rules state it is up to the individual providers whether to make their ISAs flexible or not. Even then, they can choose to restrict the flexibility to certain products and make other ISAs – such as fixed-rate products – exempt from the flexible *in, out and in* capability.

The flexibility applies to other forms of ISAs including Innovative Finance ISAs and Stocks and Shares ISAs – although you may find there are barely any providers offering this flexibility for these investment wrappers. This means that you need to check the account T&Cs before you sign up and definitely check before you make a withdrawal.

Security of cash accounts

Cash on deposit with banks and building societies is guaranteed by the Financial Services Compensation Scheme for sums of up to £85,000 in the event that the institution goes bust. The Financial Services Compensation Scheme is a government-backed but industry-funded safety net designed to give savers confidence in the UK savings system.

The level of protection has been increased significantly. A decade ago it stood at £35,000. In 2008, when banks were collapsing around the world, it was increased to £50,000. Then, at the end of 2010, it was increased again to its current level of £85,000, which is broadly in line with the €100,000 level of protection across the European Union. This level was introduced across the board to stop savers moving their cash to the countries with the highest levels of investor protection. Changes in exchange rates meant the level of protection dropped to £75,000 for a short period, although it is back up to £85,000 with effect from January 2017.

It is important to understand that savers are only entitled to one lot of £85,000 compensation per failed institution. If you have £85,000 on deposit with a bank and also have a £20,000 fixed-rate bond with that same institution, then you are exposed in the event of it going bust, as you will only get £85,000 total compensation. Savers in this situation, or who have more than £85,000 in a single bank or building society, may choose to move some of their money to a different bank, so they have no more than £85,000 per institution. If not, you could find most of your life's savings going down the drain if that bank goes bust.

Couples are each allowed £85,000-worth of protection, so joint accounts are covered up to £170,000.

A Cash ISA is treated like any other bank account for protection purposes.

The only exception to these limits is for temporarily large balances, where the FSCS will cover up to £1m per person for up to six months. This is intended to cover things like money coming in from a house sale, or from a divorce settlement, to ensure it is protected while you decide where to move it.

Merged banks – one lot of investor protection or two?

Compensation is paid up to £85,000 for each regulated institution. This means investors with assets across bank or building societies that operate under a shared regulatory licence will only get one set of cover.

Check the situation online if you have more than £85,000 with two banks. NatWest is registered as a separate institution to RBS, even though RBS owns it. So each bank is covered up to £85,000. The same applies for Lloyds and HBOS.

HSBC and First Direct, on the other hand, are registered under a single FCA licence. So anyone with £50,000 in each one will only be covered up to £85,000 and so has £15,000 of unprotected savings.

Here is a summary of banks and building societies which count as one institution:

- Barclays, Standard Life Cash Savings, The Woolwich
- Co-op Bank, Smile, Britannia
- Coventry Building Society, Stroud & Swindon
- Halifax, Bank of Scotland, Intelligent Finance, Birmingham Midshires, AA, Saga
- HSBC, First Direct
- Lloyds, Cheltenham & Gloucester
- Nationwide, Cheshire, Derbyshire, Dunfermline Building Societies
- Santander, Cahoot
- Virgin Money, Northern Rock
- Yorkshire Bank, Clydesdale Bank
- Yorkshire, Barnsley, Chelsea, Norwich & Peterborough Building Societies.

Overseas banks

Banks based within the European Union have a similar level of investor protection – €100,000.

But beware of banks that are not based in the EU as they do not have the same level of investor protection. Investors found this out the hard way when banks based in Iceland and the Isle of Man collapsed in 2008.

At the time, Icelandic banks were guaranteed by their government up to €20,887. The Isle of Man's bank deposit guarantee scheme compensated investors up to 100% of the first £30,000 and then 90% of the next £20,000 of deposits, up to a maximum of £48,000.

Cash funds

Cash funds are pooled investments run by fund managers who invest in cash-like assets with the very loose aim of giving *attractive* returns with a high level of security. They are also called *money market funds*.

These funds have come under scrutiny from the FCA in recent years because the assets they have invested in have, in some cases, not reflected the risk profile of cash. Some have also suffered from negative yields.

Cash funds are usually far less volatile than equity or bond funds but they still carry risks, and can post negative returns in times of exceptional market volatility.

Don't go into these funds for decent long-term cash returns – cash funds are purely for holding short-term cash on your investment platform while you think about where else you are going to invest it. The rates of return they generate are usually very low indeed. For example, the Scottish Widows Cash Fund, which has 0.62% annual charges, has an objective of giving you a return that's 0.05% higher than the rate at which banks borrow money, known as LIBOR. The fund's ultra-low-risk approach means that in the three years up to March 2020 it has returned -0.28%, 0.11% and 0.23% respectively.

National Savings and Investments (NS&I)

These government-backed savings products are as secure an investment as you can find. There is no reading through the small print to find out whether you are covered. They are 100% secure, to the extent that the UK government is secure, regardless of how much you hold in them.

It is no surprise, therefore, that their rates are not great. As well as offering premium bonds for those who fancy a flutter with their interest, NS&I also offers a direct Cash ISA account and a direct saver account. Neither are going to top the tables and, at the time of writing, neither savings account even beats inflation.

NS&I used to offer some very attractive products, notably fixed-interest and index-linked savings certificates. These are no longer available as they offered generous rates of return with the security of a government guarantee. For example, index-linked certificates issued in 2007 offered RPI plus 1.35%. These certificates were for a fixed period but NS&I have offered holders of the certificates the opportunity to roll them over into replacement certificates on less attractive tax-free terms (but nonetheless still reasonable in the current environment).

If you hold some of these, they probably offer better rates of interest than you will be able to get elsewhere in the market, so it is worth hanging on to them.

One advantage of National Savings Certificates is that they are completely tax-free and do not have to be declared on your tax return.

Tax on cash

Until recently, interest on cash was taxable as income, meaning you had to pay tax on it at your marginal income tax rate. Changes introduced from 6 April 2016 now mean that many savers will not pay tax on some or all of the interest they receive.

Firstly, a Personal Savings Allowance means basic-rate taxpayers don't pay tax on the first £1,000 of interest they receive. Higher rate taxpayers don't pay tax on the first £500 of interest. Additional rate taxpayers don't benefit from the Personal Savings Allowance.

Prior to the introduction of these allowances, tax of 20% was usually deducted at source from cash savings accounts. Basic-rate taxpayers had no further tax liability. If you were a higher rate or additional rate taxpayer you had to declare the income on your tax return and were required to pay the balance.

Now, because most savers won't receive interest of more than £1,000 in a tax year, interest is paid gross. Those who receive more interest than is free of tax have to declare this in a tax return.

We have covered this before, but it is worth restating that all interest on cash held in a SIPP and in an ISA is paid gross with no tax to pay. You don't have to worry about allowances in those wrappers, and any interest received doesn't count against your personal allowances.

The use of cash ISAs has dropped since the introduction of the Personal Savings Allowance, as people felt their money was protected from tax so they didn't need to use an ISA for their cash. However, it's still worth thinking about them for a couple of reasons.

First, if you move into the next tax bracket you'll see your tax-free Personal Savings Allowance slashed – in half if you go from basic-rate to higher-rate and eliminated entirely if you become an additional-rate payer. If you have a decent amount in cash this could leave you with a tax bill and too much cash to move into an ISA in one, or even two or three, tax years.

Second, future governments might change either the level of allowances under the Personal Savings Allowance or scrap it entirely, which could also leave you with a tax bill, so some people prefer to have the security of a cash ISA.

Inflation risk

Aside from the risk of the deposit-holder defaulting, covered earlier in the chapter, the other main risk from holding a lot of cash on deposit is inflation. Since 2008 it has been hard to find non-ISA accounts that will beat inflation without taking advantage of initial bonus rates, and even then, beating inflation has often not been possible. That has meant money sitting in the bank or building society has actually been shrinking in real terms.

Cash is the most secure way to hold money, but that security comes at a cost.

Cash-round-up tools

A few banks and apps will now help you to save cash each month by rounding up any transactions you make on your card and saving the difference. For example, if you spend £4.75 on your card it will round it up to £5 and put the spare 25p into a savings account. This can be a great way of saving cash without even thinking about it, and the small amounts can add up – particularly if you do most of your spending by card rather than cash.

However, watch out for where this money is being saved and any charges you incur for the service. It started out as a service from the newer app-only banks but lots of high-street names now offer it too.

Useful websites

- www.investmentsense.co.uk
- www.moneyfacts.co.uk
- www.moneysupermarket.com
- www.nsandi.com
- www.uswitch.com

14

ALTERNATIVE INVESTMENTS

While the bulk of this book discusses equities and funds to be held in an ISA, SIPP or dealing account, there are more types of investments available to the general public that can help to diversify your portfolio or play to your hobbies and interests. But be warned, some of these suggestions won't necessarily have a liquid market, meaning it could be difficult to sell when you want to.

One point worth noting is that you won't be able to invest in most of these alternatives in an ISA or SIPP. ISA rules don't allow any of these investments to be held at all. When it comes to SIPPs, prohibitively high tax charges for holding things termed as *tangible* assets – with one exception – pretty much act as a ban on holding these investments.

The focus of this chapter is those assets you can touch and feel, often referred to as alternative investments. Experts argue that alternative assets should not represent more than 10% of your overall portfolio, however, alternative investments can stir a passion in fervent supporters to the point where they invest exclusively in these asset types, convinced that their specialist knowledge gives them the edge that eludes them for more mainstream investments.

It hopefully goes without saying that these investments are unregulated, which means if they go wrong, you are on your own. But they can be far more fun to talk about at a dinner party than conventional investments.

Buy-to-let

Apart from the weather, the one thing we all love to discuss in Britain is the property market. As a nation we are fixated by house prices, DIY (not the investing type), new kitchens, nice gardens, you name it. The British dream is to own the roof over your head and then sell it for a large profit. It is therefore a natural progression to want to try to make money from other parts of the property market, be it through property rentals or other bricks and mortar-related investments.

We covered in earlier chapters how you can invest in property via a fund, REIT, listed property company or even a tracker fund. This section is about the UK's passion for owning bricks and mortar directly. In many investors' eyes, this is a mainstream, not an alternative, investment.

Investing in a property with the sole purpose of collecting a regular stream of income in the form of rent can sound very enticing. What a lot of people fail to appreciate is that you are tying up potentially large amounts of capital in a single property that may fall in value, encounter unforeseen maintenance problems, or have troublesome tenants who are always behind in paying their rent. Or worse still, the property may stay empty for long periods of time. There is no guarantee you will always have a tenant – so you may need to keep some cash up your sleeve to cover any periods when the property is unoccupied.

Buy-to-let has its pros and cons just like many other investments. When compared against the potential returns from cash savings accounts, property certainly looks a better option as long as you are prepared to deal with the extras that often come with owning it, such as boiler repairs and dealing with property management companies.

Unlike most quoted investments, you cannot sell a property and convert your capital to cash in a day or two. Many people take on debt to fund buy-to-let investments, so you need to make sure you can keep up with repayments.

Taxes are also getting much tougher for buy-to-let landlords, such as the rise in stamp duty in April 2016 and the reduction in how much of your costs you can set against your income for tax purposes. Should you eventually decide to sell, you will have to contend with capital gains tax if your property has increased in value since purchase and you've exceeded your annual £12,300 (2021/22) capital gains allowance. You have to pay an extra eight percentage points in capital gains tax on gains made through residential property when compared to gains for other investment types – basic-rate taxpayers pay 18% and higher rate taxpayers pay 28% on gains made from residential property, compared to 10% and 20% respectively on all other gains.

Any rental income, after deducting expenses, is subject to income tax at your marginal rate. Note that tax relief on mortgage interest payments has been phased out, so now no tax relief on interest payments will be available.

With all the talk about how there aren't enough houses in the UK, you could presume that rental demand will always be strong. It would be foolish, nonetheless, to believe property is a risk-free investment.

Peer-to-peer investing

Peer-to-peer, or P2P as it's commonly known, is a new area of the market to emerge after the financial crisis when banks were more reluctant to lend to businesses. The idea was for investors to cut out the middleman of the banks and lend directly to businesses, via platforms that matched up the lender and borrower. The interest rates on offer for savers were much higher than cash savings rates, particularly during such a long period of low interest rates, but were often lower for the businesses than borrowing from the bank. In theory it was a win-win.

However, there have been lots of problems with the market, after an initial boom in the number of companies offering to marry up savers and businesses and people flocking to invest. Many people perceived it as having a similar risk to cash savings (because that's often how the products were advertised) but that's emphatically not the case. You're lending to a small company, which may be successful or may fold altogether. Lots of platforms spread your money between different businesses to try to reduce this risk, and some will have contingency funds to help cover business failures, but that is not guaranteed.

The other downside that people have often realised too late is that if you need your money back it's not as easy as withdrawing it from a bank account. You'll either need another investor to effectively buy you out of your loan or you'll need to wait until the end of the loan – which can be months or years away.

The regulator has since cracked down on the market, to stop widespread advertising of the products and to limit how much money newcomer investors can put into these products. That's not to say they should be avoided, you just need to know the risks and make sure you're not putting too much of your total pot of money into peer-to-peer.

Stamps, wine, vintage cars, art and commodities

Stamps

Stamp collecting has been around in the UK since the Penny Black became the first postage stamp to be issued by Britain in 1840. While philately is perhaps not as popular as it was a hundred years ago, there are still plenty of opportunities to buy and sell stamps from around the world and potentially make a profit. The National Philately Society runs a website (see list below) that explains how to become serious about stamp collecting. You should expect any gains made from trading stamps to be subject to capital gains tax, though there are certain exemptions available that are beyond the scope of this book.

Wine

Wine collecting attracts polarised opinion. Some people say wine is for drinking; others say it can be a very lucrative investment if you know your grapes, regions and years. Unlike funds, which have an entry level of £50 per month, you will need at least £10,000 to be able to dip a toe into the world of wine investing. The demand from Asia, particularly China, has increased dramatically over recent years. But would you invest on the back of suggestions that these new-found protagonists mix wine with coke and favour red over white because the former is a lucky colour?

Take care when investing *en primeur*, a method of buying wine while it is still in the barrel and some way off being mature. It is a bit like buying a yearling at Doncaster sales – a gamble, but one that can pay off handsomely if you find the next Frankel of the wine world.

Wine should be seen as a long-term investment; my suggestion would be to spend more on a few good bottles than spreading the chips around the roulette table. Factor in storage and insurance costs – about £15 a case of six bottles per year – and make sure you store in a government-licensed bonded warehouse.

There is good news when it comes to tax. Because a bottle of wine is deemed to have a life of no more than 50 years – three days in our house – any gains are exempt from capital gains tax. But the flip side of that is you can't offset any losses on wine against gains from other investments.

As wine has become a more popular investment, new ways of accessing it have emerged, such as clubbing together with other investors, meaning you don't have to invest as much upfront, or handing the money over to experts who will hopefully increase your chances of buying the right wine that will go up in value. The detail of all these schemes is outside the scope of this book, but act with caution to make sure you're putting your money with a legitimate business.

Vintage cars

There is a healthy market for antique or rare cars, albeit this is probably restricted to the realms of the super-rich. The alternative and perhaps more affordable route is to try car restoration in order to make a profit. Vintage cars share the same tax breaks as wine, even if the vintage car is more than 50 years old.

Art

Art can be a very good investment and even quite affordable if you are prepared to invest in the works of unknown artists (as long as they subsequently find fame). Art is not classed as a wasting asset, therefore any gains may be subject to capital gains tax.

Commodities

The surge in the gold price between 2008 and 2011, from $700 to $1,900 per ounce, saw the world go potty for the precious metal. At the peak of the gold rush you would hear reports of people queuing up to buy gold coins in their lunch break. Cash for gold traders sprung up on the high street and pawnbrokers were having a field day as customers rushed to offload jewellery. Although the gold price nearly halved in value between 2012 and 2015, it has resurged again during recent times. It's the 'safety net' asset of lots of investors, so typically rises in value in uncertain times.

I have already discussed how to get exposure to commodity prices, including gold, via ETFs earlier in this book. For anyone wanting to own physical gold, the natural option would be to go to someone like the Royal Mint or a reputable coin or bullion dealer. The advantage of owning gold indirectly through an ETF is that the metal is safely stored in a vault, whereas physical ownership of coins or bars may require you to take out additional insurance or build a secure area in your basement next to your wine cellar.

Other commodities suitable for physical ownership include silver coins; buying platinum in the form of jewellery; and of course diamonds remain widely available (at a price) embedded into rings or other jewellery.

As with other tangible assets, you can't directly hold gold or silver in an ISA. SIPP rules do contain an exemption that allows investment-grade gold bullion to be held without suffering from tax charges. This exemption only applies to gold and you'll find that only SIPP providers at the bespoke end of the market will allow gold to be held.

Top websites for research and information

- www.landlords.org.uk
- www.wine-searcher.com
- www.ukphilately.org.uk
- www.gold.org
- www.royalmint.com

PART FOUR

PUTTING IT ALL TOGETHER

15

THE TAX-EFFICIENT DIY INVESTOR

There is no point being a brilliant investment-picker if you blow a chunk of your winnings through paying tax you could have avoided. Getting your tax strategy wrong can wipe out years of hard-earned investment gains, so it's essential to put your money in tax wrappers that suit your objectives.

It may not feel like it, given some of the statements coming from the government, but while tax evasion is illegal, tax avoidance is not. Avoiding tax does not necessarily mean joining the comedians, pop singers and TV stars in their aggressive offshore tax schemes – for most people it wouldn't be worth it because of the costs involved.

I adopt a simple rule when it comes to tax planning schemes. If I can find reference to it via a search engine – other than in the context of a tax case – on HMRC's website, then I will consider it. If I can't, then I won't. You will find plenty of explanatory references to all of the tax wrappers and investments covered in this book on HMRC's website.

I also subscribe to the view that you only have to pay tax when you are doing well. Paying tax is something that should be celebrated. Well, maybe that is pushing it a bit too far?

For the DIY investor, minimising tax is about the smart use of the reliefs and allowances that the government has designed to incentivise us to save for our futures. But before we get on to minimising your tax bill, you first need to understand the taxes you are looking to minimise.

The two main taxes the DIY investor needs to bear in mind are *income tax* and *capital gains tax*.

Hopefully, DIY investing will mean your assets will grow to such an extent that inheritance tax will also become an issue as you approach the end of your life. Here we focus on the two main personal taxes you will pay during your lifetime.

Income tax

You are taxed on your income in three ways, depending on the sort of income it is – general income, savings income or dividend income.

* **General income**. This is earnings from your job, whether received as an employee on a PAYE basis or income from self-employment. It also includes any rent you receive from property and income from any pension(s) you have.

* **Savings income**. This covers interest from savings accounts and deposits with banks and building societies, as well as income from gilts and qualifying corporate bonds.

* **Dividend income**. This covers income from dividends paid on your equity and fund holdings.

Table 15.1 shows the rates of tax paid on income amounts in excess of your personal allowance.

Table 15.1: Income tax rates 2020/21

Tax band	General (%)	Savings (%)	Dividend (%)
Basic rate	20	20	7.5
Higher rate	40	40	32.5
Additional rate	45	45	38.1

In addition to your personal allowance:

- The first £1,000 of savings income is tax-free for basic-rate taxpayers. For higher and additional rate taxpayers this reduces to £500 and nil respectively.

- For some lower earners there is also a £5,000 allowance, called the 'starting rate for savers' but you start to lose this once your other income goes above the personal allowance

- The first £2,000 of dividend income is tax-free in 2021/22.

Personal allowance

You only pay income tax on income above your personal allowance. These have historically been age-related but there is now a flat rate of £12,570 (2021/22) regardless of when you were born. The personal allowance rate has been frozen until 2026.

The personal allowance reduces where your income is above £100,000 – by £1 for every £2 of income above the £100,000 limit.

Income tax bands

The rate at which you pay income tax is determined by the level of your earnings above your personal allowance in that tax year.

Table 15.2: Income rate tax bands 2021/22

Rate	Earnings
Personal allowance	Up to £12,570
Basic rate 20%	£12,571–£50,270
Higher rate 40%	£50,271–£150,000
Additional rate 45%	Over £150,000

Note: for Scottish taxpayers the tax brackets are different and there are additional tax brackets at 19% and 21% and the higher and additional rate bands are 41% and 46%.

Capital gains tax

You are taxed on capital gains above the level of your annual allowance, which is £12,300 for 2021/22 for everyone, regardless of age. The capital gains tax allowance rate has been frozen until 2026. For assets other than residential property, a capital gains tax rate of 10% (18% for residential property) is payable where gains, when added to your other income, are below the higher rate threshold. A rate of 20% is charged where gains, if added to your income, are above the higher rate tax threshold.

This means, for example, someone with a £12,570 income tax personal allowance earning over £50,270 will pay a capital gains tax rate of 20% in the 2021/22 tax year. So, an individual with an income of £45,000 who has a £10,000 capital gains tax liability (above their capital gains tax annual allowance) would see the first £5,000 taxed at 10% and the balance taxed at 20% (28% for residential property).

The fact that capital gains tax is charged at a lower rate than income tax means, particularly for income-seeking higher rate taxpayers, it can be more efficient investing for growth and deriving an income by cashing in investments than by investing for income.

Table 15.3: Capital gains tax rates 2021/22

	Residential property
Basic rate taxpayers	18%
Higher and additional rate taxpayers	28%

Tax reliefs – pension and ISA

The two key ways a DIY investor will get tax relief are through pensions and ISAs.

Pension

Pension contributions paid into your SIPP benefit from tax relief at your highest rate of tax. For people paying tax at 40%, that means it costs £600 of after-tax earnings to pay £1,000 into a pension. Once in the pension, assets grow free from income and capital gains tax.

When you come to draw money from your pension, which you are normally only allowed to do after your minimum pension age, a quarter of your pot can be taken tax-free, with the balance taxed as income when it is drawn. Most people have less income in retirement than when they are working, meaning they pay less tax by tying up their money in a pension. For example, higher rate taxpayers in employment subsequently may be basic-rate taxpayers in retirement.

Traditional ISAs

Traditional ISAs do not give you tax relief when you pay money into them, which means you pay money in from your after-tax earnings. But you are relieved from income tax liability for any income they generate. Furthermore, there will be no capital gains tax liability on the growth in the assets held within the ISA wrapper.

Lifetime ISA

On 6 April 2017, a new type of ISA was introduced. The Lifetime ISA includes a tax bonus of 25% on payments of up to £4,000 made to it each year. If, for example, you were to pay the full £4,000 allowance into a Lifetime ISA in one year, the government would top this up with a bonus of £1,000.

Lifetime ISAs can only be opened by those aged between 18 and 39. If you qualify to open a Lifetime ISA, you can continue to pay money in up to the annual limit of £4,000 until the day before your 50th birthday.

One downside of the Lifetime ISA is that you'll typically pay a 25% penalty on anything you withdraw unless the proceeds are used to purchase your first residential property or they are left in the Lifetime ISA until you reach 60.

Maximising your allowances

When you come to draw money from your portfolio, you want to be able to use the tax allowances available to you to their maximum effect.

This means making the best possible use of both your income tax and capital gains tax annual allowances, wherever possible.

Maximising your capital gains tax allowance

One of the most underused tax perks has to be the annual capital gains tax exemption. By investing in assets that grow, rather than pay an income, you can make the most of this generous annual allowance.

By investing in growth assets – sometimes easier said than done – you can withdraw £12,300 (2021/22) of your capital gains each year without paying tax.

Experts warn against letting the tax tail wag the investment dog, and a diversified approach is always recommended, but by having at least some growth assets in your portfolio you will be able to draw down capital gains in years when your income tax rate is high.

Unused allowances – gifts between spouses

If you are married or in a civil partnership, you can pass assets to your other half without creating a tax liability, giving your household twice as much tax allowance to play with.

If you are still working, the chances are that your income tax allowance for the current year has been used up. But if you have a non-earning spouse or civil partner, or your spouse or partner is paying tax at a lower rate than you are, simply transfer assets into their name and you will automatically cut your tax bill.

Similarly, even if both you and your spouse or partner are earning and paying a high rate of tax, by giving them parts of your portfolio that are holding capital gains, you can both use your full £12,300 (2021/22) capital gains tax allowance – allowing you to draw £24,600 tax-free between you.

Using up spouses' and civil partners' unused allowances

The fact that gifts between spouses are free from any capital gains tax liability means it is relatively easy to move assets around to take advantage of unused ISA or SIPP allowances.

Assets attracting tax at a lower rate

Most DIY investors will stick to simply making full use of ISA and SIPP reliefs, spouse and civil partner allowances and capital gains tax allowances. But if you are paying tax at the higher or additional rate, you may want to consider some of the specialist asset classes that have been designed specifically with tax relief in mind.

The main ones are VCTs and enterprise investment schemes (EISs). At risk of repeating myself, however, you should never invest in something just because of the tax relief that is available. If you do, the underlying investment can turn out to be a dud. So treat investments that come with big headline tax advantages with caution.

16

WHEN IT ALL GOES WRONG

Nobody likes to dwell on life's negatives, but it is worth knowing what will happen to your money when significant personal events such as death, divorce or bankruptcy come along, or when you have a problem with your investment provider. These subjects are covered in this chapter.

Death and taxes

Benjamin Franklin's famous quote about death and taxes being the only things certain in life serves to underline just how important inheritance tax planning can be for your loved ones.

This is a book about DIY investing, not about estate planning, so I am going to go no further than explain what happens to the various assets a DIY investor may have built up in the event of their death.

In a nutshell, I would urge you to seek professional advice and write a will. Intestacy laws do not always lead to the outcomes you might expect, and society is full of people who have not benefited from their deceased loved one's estate in the way they had hoped they would, often causing years of resentment and hardship for those affected.

Ask yourself the question, "If I were to die tomorrow, what would happen to all my assets?" If you don't know the answer, how will your executor?

Inheritance tax

All your assets held within your ISA or dealing account will fall within your estate for inheritance tax purposes in the event of your death. This is not the case for investments held within your SIPP, which can pass to your heirs without raising an inheritance tax liability, though your beneficiaries will be liable for income tax on anything they receive if you die after reaching age 75.

When inheritance tax is payable

Inheritance tax is payable on all your assets at death above a threshold known as the *nil rate band*. The standard nil rate band is £325,000 for the tax year 2021/22. Inheritance tax on assets above the nil rate band is charged at 40%.

An additional nil rate band was introduced in April 2017 that's now worth £175,000 per person in the 2021/22 tax year. Both nil-rate bands are frozen until 2026.

The additional nil rate band is available to individuals when a residential property, which has been their residence at some point, is passed on death to a direct descendant, assuming your estate isn't worth more than £2m. It is also available to anyone who has sold their home and passes assets of an equivalent value to direct descendants on death.

Included in your estate for calculating inheritance tax are gifts made to other people, including trusts, within the previous seven years, with the tax rate reducing in tiers between 40% and zero the further the date the gift was made from the date of death. These gifts are known as *potentially exempt transfers*.

Exceptions to the inclusion of gifts in your estate are an annual gift allowance of £3,000 a year, gifts to UK-registered charities, regular gifts from income and gifts made more than seven years before you die.

Also, if you agree to leave at least 10% of your estate to one or more charities, the rate of inheritance tax on your entire estate reduces from 40% to 36%.

Spouses and civil partners

Spouses and civil partners can inherit unlimited sums from each other without having to pay any inheritance tax.

Spouses and civil partners can also inherit any unused part of the deceased's nil rate band, meaning a married couple or civil partners can always, between them, pass on at least £650,000 without paying inheritance tax. This also counts for the new residence nil rate band, meaning that a couple leaving a property can now pass on an estate worth £1m free of tax.

SIPP assets on death

Assets held in your SIPP at the time of death do not fall within your estate for inheritance tax purposes.

Death before reaching age 75

A lump sum up to your unused lifetime allowance can be paid tax-free from your SIPP in the event of your death before the age of 75. Any funds over the lifetime allowance can be paid as a cash lump sum, subject to a 55% tax charge.

If the fund is used to provide a pension to a spouse, dependant or nominee, the income is tax-free where the deceased was under 75 at the age of their death. If the fund designated to provide a pension to the beneficiary is over the lifetime allowance then a tax charge of 25% will be payable on the excess.

If you benefit from one of the various types of protection for larger funds then it may be possible for a higher amount to be paid as a lump sum or designated to a pension on death without tax being payable.

Death after age 75

If you die after you have reached age 75, a lump sum can be paid to your dependants or nominated beneficiaries. Alternatively, the whole fund can be used to provide a dependant's or nominee's pension. In either case the recipient will have to pay income tax on the funds they receive.

The tax rules on death benefits are now far more generous than they were only a few years ago. Many, your author included, are suggesting that the tax position is unsustainably generous.

It is now possible for pension funds to be passed down multiple generations with the funds kept entirely free of inheritance tax while investments are also kept free from income tax and capital gains tax.

AIM-listed shares on death

Most shares held on the AIM stock market become exempt from inheritance tax once you have held them for two years.

The AIM company must qualify for a tax break called Business Property Relief in order for the shareholder to benefit from the inheritance tax relief. Essentially it means the AIM company must generate their earnings from a proper trading business and not from investments or property.

HMRC refuses to publish a list of qualifying AIM stocks as the source of earnings can change for a business from year to year, and it has also restricted its definition of an eligible company in recent years to stop widespread use of this tax break. This is a more complicated topic than you might imagine and anyone buying AIM stocks specifically for their inheritance tax benefits should seek advice from a tax specialist. The alternative is to use the services of an AIM portfolio manager as they generally consult accountants or tax experts to assess qualification of the stocks in their portfolio.

Divorce

All your investments, including your SIPP holdings, will be taken into account by the court in the event that you and your spouse or civil partner divorce.

The court can order SIPP and other pension assets to remain in your name and be offset against other assets retained by the other party. Alternatively, the court can also order your SIPP to be split between you and your former spouse, a procedure known as *pension sharing*.

An ISA or a dealing account is treated like any other asset in a divorce. You should note that there is no equivalent concept to pension sharing where you can pass an ISA intact between two divorcing parties.

Bankruptcy

In the event that you are declared bankrupt, the trustee in bankruptcy (TIB) appointed to administer your affairs will be able to take control of all your investment assets, except for those held in your pension where special rules apply. If you are declared bankrupt, or think you are likely to be, seek specialist advice.

Up until recently, the position was that a TIB could not access pension benefits where benefits hadn't commenced. Where benefits had commenced, then the TIB could use pensions in payment to satisfy creditors.

Several recent court cases have raised the possibility that the TIB could force access to a pension fund, even where the bankrupt had yet to start taking benefits.

The *Raithatha* v *Williamson* court case ruled that the TIB could force Mr Williamson to commence benefits and then use the proceeds to satisfy his creditors. The appeal was settled out of court, so what appeared to many of us to be a flawed judgement looked as though it would cause concern for some time.

More recently, the court case *Horton v Henry* has contradicted the *Raithatha v Williamson* decision. The *Horton v Henry* case did go to appeal and the judge made it very clear that he found the decision in *Raithatha v Williamson* to be flawed. This appears to mean anyone over the age of 55 who is made bankrupt will not see their pension benefits taken by the TIB, but we'll have to wait and see whether any more cases go before the court before we can be absolutely certain.

How to complain about your investment platform

Most investment platforms do a pretty good job, but you may find that service falls below the standards to which you are entitled. A strongly worded letter to the platform may sort out your problem, but if you are still not satisfied then you are entitled to take your complaint to the proper authority, as explained below.

ISA, dealing account and SIPP complaints

Complaints about your dealing account, ISA and SIPP should be made to the Financial Ombudsman Service, or the Financial Services Compensation Scheme (FSCS), a government-backed organisation, in the event that the platform or SIPP provider has ceased trading.

For SIPPs, if your complaint is about maladministration you can complain to the Pensions Ombudsman.

Product and provider insolvency and the FSCS

There is always the possibility that one or more of the investment product providers that you use will go bust. Some but not all financial products are protected by the FSCS.

In general terms, the FSCS covers UK-based deposits, investments and insurance policies. Deposits and investments are covered up to £85,000. Joint accounts benefit from double these figures. Insurance products are covered up to 100% or 90% of their value, however great it is, depending on the type of insurance

Cash on deposit in a bank or building society

Bank and building society deposits are guaranteed by the FSCS for sums of up to £85,000 in the event that an institution goes bust. You are protected up to the level of £85,000 per failed institution and two banks that have merged may be treated as a single bank for the purposes of the FSCS.

Cash on deposit on an investment platform

If the bank your investment platform uses goes bust then you are entitled to compensation up to the FSCS limit of £85,000.

Investment platforms often deposit cash with more than one bank, so it is not possible to monitor this with a view to making sure that you stay within the £85,000 limit with any one bank. Although not tested legally, it is the widely held view that the £85,000-per-person limit would apply to each bank that your investment platform holds its cash with – meaning the more banks it holds cash with, the more protection you have.

Fund manager insolvency

Unit trust and OEIC managers are required by the regulator to put your investments with a trustee or depository rather than actually holding them themselves in their own name. So, if a fund manager does become insolvent then your unit trusts and OEICs would not be affected.

It is just about conceivable that the trustee or depositary used by the fund manager could become insolvent, but we are talking about the very biggest financial organisations in the world, and if they were to go bust the whole global financial system would be in meltdown. Most professionals do not see trustee or depository default as a genuine risk.

In the event of loss caused by a fund manager through negligence or fraud, the FSCS pays compensation up to £85,000 per person per provider.

ETF default

To date, no ETF or other exchange-traded product has ever gone into default, but technically it could happen. Like funds, ETFs place the assets on trust on your behalf with a nominee, meaning they are ring-fenced. If the ETF provider became insolvent, your assets would be protected from its creditors.

Synthetic and leveraged ETFs that use derivatives to pay multiples of the rise or fall in an index could find themselves unable to pay out in the event that the counterparty behind the derivative went bust. But UCITS rules require ETFs domiciled in the EU to have no more than

10% of the fund's value exposed to a single counterparty risk, so the failure of a counterparty should not be fatal.

Most ETFs are domiciled overseas, in countries such as Luxembourg or Ireland, but even those domiciled in the UK are not protected by the FSCS.

Investment trusts

Investment trusts are simply limited companies whose value goes up and down in line with the market's attitude to the value of the shares they hold. They are not regulated products and therefore do not benefit from FSCS protection.

But there are occasions when compensation can be payable in relation to investment trusts, as happened following the split-cap investment trust scandal at the start of the century. Compensation was available from the FSCS where investors lost money when they were misled into buying a product that was unsuitable, or where the risks of the investment were not fully explained and that loss resulted from the actions of a regulated organisation.

Unregulated collective investment schemes (UCISs)

As their name suggests, unregulated collective investment schemes (UCISs) do not, of themselves, benefit from the protection of the FSCS. Compensation can be payable if you are mis-sold one by a regulated firm, such as a financial adviser. But if you invest in a UCIS as a DIY investor you will be doing so on an *execution-only* or buyer beware basis, which means you will have no recourse in the event that your money disappears for any reason.

Equities

If a company in which you hold shares goes bust, you will lose some or all of your money. A liquidator will be appointed and, once all creditors have been paid, the remaining funds (if there are any) will be shared out among shareholders equally. There is no FSCS protection.

Bonds

Bondholders rank ahead of shareholders but behind secured creditors in the event of a company's insolvency. But, like equities, corporate bonds do not benefit from FSCS protection.

Corporate bonds should be distinguished from fixed-rate bonds issued by banks and building societies, which do benefit from FSCS protection up to £85,000.

Investment platform insolvency

All investments, including cash held by your investment platform on your behalf, are segregated from the platform's own assets. This means that if your investment platform goes bust then your money will not be affected, although you may have to wait a little longer to get access to it.

Venture capital trusts and enterprise investment schemes

Neither venture capital trusts (VCTs) nor enterprise investment schemes (EISs) benefit from FSCS protection. If the VCT or EIS loses all its money you will not be able to claim any compensation. But if the fund manager running it goes bust and owes you money, and it is regulated and therefore covered by the FSCS, you will be able to claim compensation of up to £85,000 per person.

Useful websites

- www.financial-ombudsman.org.uk
- www.fscs.org.uk
- www.pensionsadvisoryservice.org.uk
- www.pensions-ombudsman.org.uk

17

BUILDING A RISK-ADJUSTED PORTFOLIO

Being a DIY investor is not just about picking the top shares or funds in a particular sector. You also need to understand which sectors to invest in, and what proportion of your portfolio to put in them. This process is called asset allocation, and it is a crucial factor in building a DIY investment portfolio.

Generally speaking, the greater the investment return you want to achieve, the greater the risk you will need to take. But the longer the time frame you set, the greater the chance you will achieve your investment objectives.

Investments can go down as well as up. We all know that, but some investments are more volatile than others. Different risks attach themselves to different investments. The biggest risk to investing in cash is not the bank going bust, but inflation. Investing in corporate bonds is typically regarded as being safer than investing in equities, though as we have seen in Chapter 12, these investments are not immune to sharp price movements.

Risks are most concentrated in the individual investments you choose to buy, but there is also the risk that the vehicle in which you use to hold your investments could turn out to be the wrong one. For example, you could invest the bulk of your savings in a SIPP, only to find you really need access to your money before the age of 55. Maybe investing in an ISA would have been a better option.

Other risks you need to think about include living too long – strange as that may sound – or the possibility that you might become critically ill, and any number of other significant and unexpected changes in your personal circumstances.

Investment experts will always tell you that asset allocation is more important to your overall portfolio returns than fund manager or share selection. For example, by investing solely in UK-focused equities or funds you are nailing your colours to the UK economy. If that goes down, your investments go with it. Not only that, but you will miss out on the potentially greater growth elsewhere, such as from emerging markets, bonds, corporate property, commodities, US equities or whichever other sector is having its day in the sun.

Markets are cyclical, with different sectors rising and falling at different points in the economic cycle. Watching everything you have go down in value all at the same time is enough to test the most resolute of long-term investors, and risks tempting you to bail out at the bottom of the market – which is, of course, the worst possible thing to do. By spreading your risk across different asset classes you can smooth out the peaks and troughs, making it psychologically that much easier to stay the course.

Attitude to, or appetite for, risk is very personal and I do find some people are guilty of over-analysing risk, while others just pay it lip service. There is a happy medium.

What is risk?

Risk is a difficult thing to explain or assess objectively. We all know that shares may go down in value as well as up. Corporate bonds are less risky than shares, meaning they are less likely to go down in value but also less likely to go up. Cash on deposit only goes up (except if you take account of inflation), but it is likely to go up more slowly than corporate bonds or equities. And that is the point with risk – there is no guarantee that any particular outcome is going to happen, positive or negative.

All you can say about the risk profile of different asset classes is what they are more or less likely to deliver. Equities are meant to outperform bonds and cash over the long term, yet in the first decade of the new millennium they didn't.

But the fact that risks sometimes don't pay off shouldn't mean you just leave all your money in cash. Because not taking any risk also has its risks – the risk of missing out on bigger returns, and of seeing your cash eroded by inflation. This is a phenomenon known as *reckless caution*, and, usually, the less a person understands about investments and economics, the more likely they are to suffer from it.

Cash is the least risky investment class, followed by bonds, property and then equities.

Some key risks to consider:

- **Inflation risk**. If your investment return is less than inflation, the real value of your investments will be eroded. This is particularly relevant for cash and bond investments.

- **Economic and political risk**. Your investments are likely to be impacted by significant economic or political events. Economic issues that may impact on the return you get from your investments include interest rates, growth of the economy, levels of employment, inflation and political upheaval. When governments increase interest rates, for example to tackle inflation, it will often result in a fall in the value of bonds and possibly also a fall in the value of equities.

- **Personal circumstances risks**. Your personal circumstances will most probably change over time and you need to try to anticipate these changes. It is not always easy to do this, and some of these risks may be dealt with by insurance rather than by adapting your investment strategy.

- **Credit or default risk**. This is most relevant when investing in corporate bonds and government bonds, but every investment carries some level of risk that the issuer may go bust. Some but not all investments are protected by the Financial Services Compensation Scheme (covered in more detail in Chapter 16).

- **Shortfall risk**. You need to consider the possibility that you don't meet your investment objectives within the time frame you have set yourself, and so are left short on the money that you needed.

- **Currency risk**. If you live in the UK and invest in only UK-denominated assets then you won't need to worry about currency risk. But if you are saving to repay a mortgage on your holiday home in Spain or if you invest in foreign shares, bonds and funds from the UK, then this is a very real risk.

- **Liquidity risk**. This is most relevant when investing in obscure investments and relates to how long it will take you to offload assets when you need to sell. You need to ensure you can easily sell your investment when you need the cash.

- **Sector risk**. One sector may perform very badly and unless you have a well-diversified portfolio this could really hit your total investment return.

- **Tax risk**. Tax rules will change over time and you need to ensure that you keep abreast of these changes to ensure you maintain a tax-efficient investment strategy.

Like you did with your investment objectives, try writing down some of the risks you are worried about, using the examples and the risk-profiling tools mentioned here.

Next to each risk, write down your risk appetite. This may be on a scale of 1 to 6, where 1 is when you want minimal risk and 6 is you are happy to be cavalier and accept the consequences. Or you may just rank your appetite for risk as low, low-medium, medium-high or high. I try to avoid using an odd number of ranking categories as it is just too tempting to opt for the middle one.

Here are some issues to consider when going through this process. You can adapt this list to include any of the other risks mentioned above that are relevant to you:

Table 17.1: Risk and risk appetite

Risk	Appetite for risk
Capital value falling by 0–10%	
Capital value falling by 10–20%	
Capital value falling by 20–50%	
Income falling by 0–10%	
Income falling by 10–20%	
Income falling by 20–50%	
Objectives target missing deadline by:	
< 1 year	
1–3 years	
3–5 years	
Objectives target missing amount by:	
0–5%	
5–10%	
10–20%	
I live to 120	
I am ill and can no longer work	
Property prices shoot up (I am saving for a house deposit)	
University fees shoot up (I am investing for my kids' tuition fees)	
I lose my job	

When considering your appetite for any of the risks above, it helps to think in the context of the opportunity cost. So, for example, when considering how you score the risk of your capital value falling by 0–10%, counter any natural inclination to score it as an unacceptable risk by thinking of the flip side opportunity – which is your capital value increasing by an equal amount. If you cannot stomach the thought of any fall at all in the value of your invested capital, then this process will have done its job – it will have shown you are not a DIY investor.

Your attitude to risk

Attitude to risk is a deeply personal thing, influenced by your psychological make-up, your experiences of gain or loss, and your sense of security in the world.

We all want *as much as possible* from our investments, but we are not all prepared to take the same level of risk to get a particular return.

This means it is not possible to create a one-size-fits-all asset allocation model for everybody. So it is important to go for an asset allocation strategy that reflects your personality. There are a number of tools to help you work this out.

Risk-profiling tools

There are several good risk-profiling tools available free on the internet. There is a very simple one on the Standard Life website. Put 'Standard Life risk profiler' into a search engine to find it quickly. After answering ten quick questions about your attitude to losing money and seeing investments rise and fall in value, you will be given one of five rankings.

I also like the high-level risk profiler available on the Vanguard website. This questionnaire is designed for the American market, so talks from a US perspective, but you can easily fill it in on the basis of switching UK for USA. This profiler also goes a step further and gives you a rough asset allocation split for your objectives.

Your investment objectives

The amount of risk you can afford to take will depend on the length of time you are planning to tie up your money. The risks of the stock market mean you should not really be investing in equities over the short term.

As a general rule, the longer your investment horizon, the more risk you can afford to take. It is also generally the case that the more money you have, the more risk you can afford to take. These two rules should be borne in mind when considering the guidelines set out below.

CNN Money has a useful asset allocation calculator:
www.money.cnn.com/tools/assetallocwizard/assetallocwizard.html

It is again designed for Americans but it is fully transportable to the UK. For example, with a time horizon of ten to 20 years and a medium appetite for risk, it suggests a portfolio made up of:

- Large-cap stocks – 35%

- Bonds – 25%

- Small-cap stocks – 20%

- Overseas stocks – 20%

In all likelihood, as a DIY investor you need not follow these portfolio construction ideas to the letter, or rather the number. The more complex ones are generally designed for high-net-worth individuals with a lot of money. As long as you get a decent level of diversification, across a handful of sectors, your portfolio will be in the right ballpark.

These portfolios, constructed from equities, ETFs, OEICs, investment trusts, bonds and gilts, are suitable for your core investment holdings. Once you have your bedrock investments in place in a balanced portfolio, you may start to feel adventurous and experiment with less mainstream asset classes.

Medium-term investing

If you are investing over the medium term, say five to ten years, you should be considering a higher proportion of equities, but you should not be investing as aggressively as long-term investors.

Sometimes it pays to invest in a similar asset to the thing you are saving up to buy. For example, imagine if you saved for a house deposit for five years, hit your savings target and then found that property prices have doubled, meaning you couldn't buy the sort of property you had planned to. By putting some of your portfolio into a residential property fund that provides exposure to the price of UK residential property, at least part of your investment pot would increase in line with your target.

Long-term investing

For periods over ten years and stretching into decades you may be able to afford to be increasingly risky in your investment strategy, whether in your SIPP or through assets you can access at any stage of your life. You should not go for risky investments just for the sake of it, but you can afford to take higher risks that reward you with higher returns.

This means a greater exposure to global equities, whether through funds or ETFs. Actively managed global equity funds can target opportunities in countries where economic growth is greater. The longer your investment horizon, the more you can invest in emerging markets.

Income investing in retirement

While risky assets such as emerging markets are fine for your pension or other retirement savings when there is still a long time before you will be drawing an income, they are generally not a good idea when you are actually in retirement.

As you approach your retirement, you may want to transform the make-up of your portfolio from an aggressive growth strategy to an income strategy. This means gradually switching portions of your fund from riskier asset classes, such as emerging markets, smaller companies and technology stocks, towards corporate bonds, government bonds, dividend-paying blue-chip stocks and cash.

If you need absolute certainty of income in retirement then you can buy an annuity from an insurance company. But doing so is a once-in-a-lifetime deal you make with an insurer, and you will be stuck with whatever income they give you for life.

Annuities are now very unpopular, not least because your capital is lost on death and because increases in longevity have meant the rates they pay out are half what they were 15 years ago. Annuity rates have been depressed further by low interest rates and extremely onerous capital adequacy requirements on insurers, meaning that you are effectively investing in a product that tracks government bonds.

Split between asset classes

There are many different rules of thumb when it comes to asset allocation, such as the rule that your equity exposure, as a percentage, should be 100 minus your age. That may work for some, but it doesn't tell you what the remainder should be in. There are many diverse views on asset allocation splits and there is clearly no right answer.

I have deliberately avoided straying into suggesting what sectors you should and shouldn't invest in, as this changes daily. But Table 17.2 provides examples of typical risk-adjusted asset allocations.

Table 17.2: Risk-adjusted asset locations

	UK equities	Global equities	Bonds	Property	Commodities	Cash
Higher risk/ aggressive	30%	38%	10%	15%	5%	2%
Medium to higher risk/ moderately aggressive	30%	35%	15%	15%	2%	3%
Medium risk/ balanced	25%	30%	30%	10%	0%	5%
Lower to medium risk/ cautious	25%	20%	35%	10%	0%	10%
Lower risk/ defensive	25%	15%	45%	0%	0%	15%

You can find actively managed funds covering the above sectors by searching on any of the websites referred to at the end of Chapter 8. If you want to find a tracker fund then the easiest way to find one that covers the market or index you want to invest in is to visit the website of one of the large ETF providers highlighted in Chapter 9.

If you put ten investment advisers in a room, they will come up with at least ten asset allocations for any given situation. Without the benefit of hindsight, none are right and none are wrong.

For the novice investor who doesn't have much time to research individual investments, it is hard to argue against a portfolio of low-cost tracker funds.

A well-diversified portfolio for someone investing over the medium/long term for capital growth with a medium-high risk appetite may look something like Table 17.3.

Table 17.3: A well-diversified portfolio of investments

Index	Percentage weighting	Notes
UK equity – FTSE All-Share Index	35%	Tracks the UK's largest listed companies, representing around 98% of the capitalisation of the whole market.
Global equity – FTSE Developed ex-UK Index	25%	Tracks the performance of all the developed equity markets in the world, excluding UK.
Corporate bonds – Global Aggregate Corporate Bond Index	20%	Provides a broad-based measure of the global investment-grade corporate bond fixed-rate debt market.
Emerging markets – MSCI Emerging Markets Index	10%	Tracks emerging markets in Europe, Asia, Africa, Latin America and Russia.
UK property – FTSE EPRA/NAREIT UK Index	10%	Tracks UK-listed real estate companies and real estate investment trusts (REITS).

There are, of course, very many variations of the above, but you will see that it is a diversified portfolio that can be put together in literally minutes.

Rebalancing your portfolio

There are two reasons why you will need to revisit the asset allocation of your portfolio at regular intervals. First because markets change and experts' views of what a sensible asset allocation strategy actually is can change, and secondly because growth or losses in certain parts of your portfolio can leave it unbalanced. This means you need to monitor the relevance of your asset allocation strategy at least every couple of years, and ideally annually.

When you do this you also need to think about 'concentration risk' with one fund or fund manager. If a fund manager has done particularly well you could end up with a disproportionate amount of your portfolio with that one person. You might be happy with that all the time they are handing out stellar performance, but you're introducing more risk into your portfolio. If the manager hits a rocky patch, their style goes out of favour, they leave the company or, worse, get hit by a bus, then more of your portfolio will be affected by that one change than you may like.

It's psychologically hard to sell some of your assets with a manager that is continuing to perform, but your future self could thank you for it should the worst happen.

Correlation

When looking at different asset classes and sectors, it is helpful to understand how they may be correlated. Some are positively correlated – that is, they tend to move in the same direction at the same time. Others are negatively correlated, where a fall in the value of one asset class is normally accompanied by a rise in the other. Or they can be uncorrelated, meaning they move in different directions at different points in time. Correlation is measured on a continuous scale between –1, a perfect negative correlation, 0 where there is no correlation, and 1 where there is perfect positive correlation.

Figure 17.1 shows the correlation between some major asset classes.

Figure 17.1: Correlation between major asset classes, July 2004 to June 2007

	UK equities	Global equities	UK gilts	Global govt. bonds	UK corp. bonds	Commods.
UK equities		0.98	-0.44	-0.15	-0.23	0.60
Global equities	0.98		-0.55	-0.27	-0.34	0.62
UK gilts	-0.44	-0.55		0.81	0.91	-0.47
Global govt. bonds	-0.15	-0.27	0.81		0.89	-0.26
UK corp. bonds	-0.23	-0.34	0.91	0.89		-0.30
Commods.	0.60	0.62	-0.47	-0.26	-0.30	

Source: *Shares* Magazine

You will see that UK equities and global equities have the highest positive correlation, whereas UK equities and UK gilts have the largest negative correlation.

A final thought on risk and portfolio construction

There is a lot of analysis about model portfolios and portfolio construction, much of which you will choose to ignore. My golden rule, above all others, is to diversify. Spread your assets across several sectors, investment types and also between different fund managers and you are less likely to come unstuck than someone who puts everything they have on a punt on a specific sector of the market.

18

STRATEGIES FOR INVESTING

In the previous chapter we looked at ways of measuring your personal appetite for risk and how to use that information to decide how to spread your investments across different asset classes – a process known as portfolio construction.

But knowing which asset classes to invest in only gets you halfway there. It's not just a question of where to invest, but also how you go about it. And this comes down to knowing what investment style is right for you.

As a DIY investor, you have to choose how to approach investing in the asset classes you have decided to target – whether through directly held equities, bonds, gilts and other assets, or through funds. Once you have decided whether you are going to invest directly or through funds, you then need to decide the level of ongoing active input you want, whether from yourself or from a fund manager.

There are lots of different strategies for investing, many of which are too complex to do justice to here, though if you are interested there are many good books that cover this topic in greater detail.

This book is aimed at people who want to invest for their future and then get on with the rest of their lives, not those who want to become part-time or full-time investors. So I have only covered the main strategies here and I have deliberately not gone into frequent-dealing strategies or day trading in any great detail. These are highly complex areas and would fill a book on their own.

There is no definitive answer to the question 'Which is the best strategy?'. Many people, myself included, use more than one strategy across their portfolio and, as you will see, some of the strategies overlap.

The fund investor

If you haven't got the time or the inclination to research individual stocks and monitor them on an ongoing basis, then being a fund investor is right for you. You're effectively outsourcing the day-to-day hassle and time of monitoring each company to a fund manager. But, it's not entirely hands-off, you still need to select your fund manager wisely and with a thorough research process and you do need to continue to monitor them, to make sure they're investing how you'd expect. But if you allocate money to a fund manager who in turn invests in 50 companies, for example, you only have to monitor one person rather than all 50 underlying holdings.

National newspapers, specialist investment magazines and various investment websites have loads of great articles on which funds to buy and sell. You can easily see what areas financial advisers and other DIY investors are recommending by visiting the Investment Association's website, which shows the best and worst-selling sectors each month. Many investment platforms have a top buy and sell list for funds and equities, which tracks what other customers are doing. There is no shortage of information on funds and it is just about finding a source that you like and trust. Just make sure that you do enough research – don't just rely on one source telling you a fund manager or fund is good and buying off the back of that.

The frequent trader

Everyone likes the idea of easy money. Buying shares, waiting a short period for them to rise in value and selling them at a healthy profit sounds like a great strategy. If only it were that easy.

Making money out of buying and selling shares requires a lot of commitment and effort and should not form the sole focus of your long-term savings. If you know a company well and think its fundamentals mean it should be valued more highly than it actually is, then yes, you may well make money out of it. And if you fancy trying to get rich quick, good luck. But be aware of the risks.

If you think frequent trading of shares is for you, then do plenty of research before you start investing.

Another good way to hone your skills before you start playing the markets with real cash is virtual investing – like fantasy football only with shares. There are a number of websites that will let you trade virtual money rather than lose your own cash learning the ropes. One of the best of these is BullBearings (www.bullbearings.co.uk).

If you are a frequent trader, then your selection of investment platform will be crucial. If you are making a lot of trades, then the amount you pay per deal will really start to add up and will eat into your profits. The last thing you want is to make a healthy return and then discover you've handed over half of it in trading costs. But the real killer is stamp duty, which is 0.5% of the purchase price of each equity investment.

The day trader

Day trading is definitely only for the committed experts.

Day trading was born off the back of the dot-com bubble at the end of the 1990s, when soaring share prices became the very definition of easy money. People started throwing in their day jobs to make a living trading short movements in share prices, until the bubble burst on the turn of the millennium, after which markets promptly went into a nosedive for a couple of years.

We didn't hear anything about day traders for a while thereafter, but then newspaper articles about them started to re-emerge as memories faded and markets recovered. The point is, very few day traders manage to make money at all stages in the investment cycle. If you want to chance your arm as a day trader, good luck to you. There are plenty of websites and books that will claim to show you how, but most tend to find that the costs of buying and selling more than outweigh any gains they can make.

Market information

Market information is a key factor to bear in mind when buying shares. You are pitting your wits against professional fund managers. If Warren Buffett is selling shares that you are buying, I know who I would back – no offence intended.

But it is fair to say that DIY investors may have the opportunity to beat the professional fund manager by investing in company shares, either those listed on AIM or those LSE-quoted companies capitalised at sub-£1bn. This is where the chat rooms, social media discussions, tip sheets and specialist financial magazines tend to focus their energies.

Specialist investment magazines and websites, such as *Shares* or *Investors Chronicle*, provide weekly market and company information, as well as a number of share tips.

Websites such as Stockopedia provide lots of research information on individual listed companies, and the bulletin boards such as London South East provide personal observations and reviews.

Some investors like to track whether directors of listed companies are buying or selling shares in their own company – as they will hopefully know more about the company than the market will.

There are strict rules surrounding when directors can buy and sell shares, and often there may be a very innocent reason. For example, a director may decide to cash in share options that have just matured or they may cash in money to buy a new house. However, a beleaguered chief executive may buy shares to try and help swing market sentiment back in the company's favour. In the main, though, directors buying or selling shares in their own companies is a good indicator, and one that many investors will follow.

One way to follow directors' share purchases and sales and search for specific activity is using the Director Deals sections of www.sharesmagazine.co.uk.

The long-term buy and hold investor

This, combined with passive investing, explained below, is arguably the strategy that gives the DIY investor the best chance of good returns for minimum effort over a long period of time.

Buy and hold investing is founded on the idea that markets will give a good rate of return in the long term, in the way that they have done over long periods for most of the past 100 or so years. Buy and hold investors believe it isn't possible to beat the market by making short-term bets on swings in valuations because the increased costs of dealing, including broker costs, stamp duty and bid/offer spreads, will more often than not wipe out whatever gains, if any, the investor trying to time the market might make.

Supporters of buy and hold investing argue that markets are efficient, so that the price of a share is always accurate, meaning there is no scope for an investor to find undervalued shares. This theory is known as the *efficient market hypothesis*, which you could research more about elsewhere if you wanted to.

Investment legend Warren Buffett, chairman and chief executive of investment giant Berkshire Hathaway, is a buy and hold investor of sorts in that he holds stocks for a very long time and keeps portfolio turnover to a minimum. We will see later in this chapter that Warren Buffett is also often categorised as a value investor, an example of the overlap of two different strategies.

The passive investor

The passive investor has no confidence that fund managers actually add value, and instead opt for the cheaper option of buying investments that just track the performance of a market or index. If this is an argument that chimes with you, then you are in the company of a growing band of financial advisers, DIY investors and other investment experts.

There have been many surveys that support this argument, though I still believe that the best managers will deliver the goods more often than not.

The real trick in passive investing is choosing the right index to track. Once you have done this, if you stick with a low-cost mainstream tracker fund provider you won't go far wrong. As I mentioned above, you can use some passive investments in your portfolio alongside active funds or direct stock picking – it doesn't have to be all or nothing.

The momentum investor

In its simplest form, a momentum investor buys investments that are on the rise and sells investments that are falling in value. Without stating the obvious, in times of rising markets this strategy works well but when markets are falling, it can be disastrous. There is a bit of momentum investor in all of us. We are often attracted to an investment or market sector because it is doing well and hope we have joined the ride early enough to make some money.

The regular investor

Regular investing is a great way of building up a pot of money over time, but you need to keep an eye on the costs of doing this.

Most platforms offer a regular investment service, which lets you pay in a small amount of money each month. The aim is to make investing more accessible to people who haven't got a large lump sum to put into markets. At the time of writing, the typical fee in the market is £1.50 per trade if you set up a regular investment.

A £1.50 fee on £1,000 investment equates to a 0.15% charge. If you were investing £100 a month that figure would jump to 1.5% and clearly it would be good to get that figure lower. However, regular investing could be a good way to get you in the savings habit, even if you can't afford to invest much to begin with.

There's another benefit to regular investing, in that you're not putting all your money into the market at one time. Anyone investing a lump sum has the worry that there could be a large fall in investment values just around the corner. By drip-feeding money, you stagger your investments so if the stock market does fall you'll only have invested some of your savings and your next investment will benefit from the cheaper share prices available. Over time you benefit from what is called pound-cost averaging, which we covered briefly in Chapter 2.

The majority of platforms let you pick the main UK stocks, funds, investment trusts and ETFs in their regular investment service.

Funds may suit regular savers better than individual shares. This is partly down to the fact that dealing costs may be cheaper but also because you can get greater diversification.

Some investment platforms even have ready-made portfolios that you can invest in via their regular investment scheme.

The income investor

Income investing is a strategy for people at a point in their lives when they want to start drawing income from their assets, while preserving capital, rather than growing their fund. Typically, those who have reached retirement make up a big part of this group, but it would also apply to those who want to use their investments to supplement their income.

Income investors face a number of big challenges, and changes to interest rates and inflation are but two. Today's low-interest rate environment is forcing income investors to look beyond cash to riskier but higher-yielding asset classes.

They also face the added challenge of generating sufficient income without excessively eroding their capital, which is the income generation engine room. If the capital goes, the income goes with it.

Spreading risk is one of the most basic principles of financial planning, and there is nothing wrong with also apportioning a small part of your portfolio to slightly racier bond-like assets such as preference shares or permanent interest-bearing shares, which can pay higher incomes. But don't bet too much on these asset classes unless you can afford to suffer losses if things go wrong.

You can search for the highest-yielding shares in the UK through websites such as Stockopedia and SharePad. Be aware, though, a high dividend yield may be masking other problems with a company, so don't buy on the basis of yield alone.

If you don't want the hassle of having to choose which corporate bonds or high-yielding equities to buy, there are plenty of funds out there to serve your needs.

High-yielding equities may offer a level of protection against inflation that corporate bonds do not, but they also expose you to far more volatility. If we enter another bear market, their value will usually fall more than your corporate bonds. So it makes sense to spread your risk by spreading your holdings between equity income funds and corporate bond funds.

How much risk you can afford to take for the level of return you want will also dictate the sort of bond holdings you go for. Investment-grade bond funds are more secure than high-yield bond funds, but the returns tend to be lower.

If you simply cannot afford any risk that your income isn't paid, then you need to source the best fixed-rate deposits you can find. Generally speaking, the longer you are prepared to tie up your money, the higher the interest rate.

The growth investor

Growth investing is, as you've doubtless guessed, investing to maximise the value of your portfolio, rather than to achieve a steady income.

In its purest form it means going for companies that look to reward investors by increasing their share price by growing their market capitalisation, rather than paying dividends. That means targeting companies that are at a relatively early stage in their development, such as tech companies, rather than mature blue-chip companies that pay steady dividends.

Technology stocks have been seen as the classic growth stocks for years, rewarding investors with increases in share price rather than dividends. But you can't avoid being a mature company forever, and Apple's decision in 2012 to pay a dividend for the first time since 1995 was seen as a turning point in its development. The same applies to easyJet, which caved in to shareholder pressure to ease back on constantly buying new planes and start paying dividends back in 2010.

Stocks targeted by growth investors often appear expensive in terms of their price-to-earnings or price-to-book ratio. This is because their share price reflects investors' belief in the future earnings potential of the company through its future growth. Good examples of this are emerging markets and commodities-related stocks that are priced on an expectation of continued growth in demand for their services because of the overarching emerging markets growth story.

Smaller companies can be fertile ground for the DIY growth investor. A company with a market cap of £50m has a lot more chance of doubling in value than giants like HSBC or BP. Many frequent traders follow a growth investing strategy, researching the companies they are interested in, banking gains when they come along and then moving on to the next opportunity.

The value investor

Value investing involves buying shares in companies that appear to be undervalued in the belief that market forces will eventually force up their value to their natural level.

Value investing is said by many to be the opposite of growth investing. But value flag-bearer, and arguably the most celebrated investor of our times, Warren Buffett, would disagree. Buffett is on record as saying the two are "joined at the hip". He is also described as a buy and hold investor, as he is not a great believer in short-term speculation.

If you are interested in reading first-hand how this value-investing legend communicates with his investors each year, go to www.berkshirehathaway.com/letters/letters.html.

Value strategies

Value investors look for shares in companies that have low price-to-earnings (PE) ratios or low price-to-book ratios. Academic studies have repeatedly shown that value stocks outperform growth stocks over the long term.

But critics of value investing point out this is not always the case, as happened in the late 1990s. These critics also point out that there is no set way to value a stock, and that two analysts might come to a different valuation.

Even so, the basic tenet of value investing – that companies that are cheap in relation to the amount of earnings they return should be a good bet in the long term – is very persuasive. And given it works for a large number of successful managers in the UK, it is a strategy DIY investors may want to follow.

In the UK, you can access funds that operate a value-investing strategy through many of the successful equity income managers.

Stockopedia and SharePad's stock screening facilities allow you to search for growth and value stocks, as well as high-yielding ones.

The ethical investor

Tobacco, gambling, weapons, alcohol, animal testing, pornography, child labour, fossil fuels – the list of activities some investors find unpalatable is long and varied. If you do not like the idea of putting your money into funds that invest in activities that go against your principles, there are plenty of funds available to meet your needs. But you need to make sure you get the right fund for your ethical principles. These strategies have boomed in popularity in recent years as more investors have flocked to them, which means there's much more choice out there for the ethical investor but it also means there are more strategies and approaches to sift through.

Funds are typically described as light green or dark green, depending on the extent to which they adhere to ethical principles.

- **Light green funds**. Avoid companies deriving a high proportion of revenue from animal testing, pornography, tobacco and weapons manufacture.

- **Dark green funds**. Adopt a stricter approach, which often excludes companies that have any interest at all in areas ethical investors have issues with. They often seek out companies making a positive contribution to society and the environment.

As the industry has grown, lots of different strategies have evolved, so it's not enough to buy a fund badged as ethical or 'ESG' (environmental, social and governance) as you might discover when you dig deeper that it actually invests in all the companies you'd be horrified to have in your portfolio. Some funds prefer to buy into the so-called 'harmful' companies so they have a seat at the table to push for change, while others will avoid them like the plague. You just need to work out what suits your own preferences and find a good fit. Also, as more money has flocked to ethical strategies more fund managers are trying to gain a piece of that pie, so be careful of those funds that call themselves ethical but only pay lip-service to actually investing ethically.

A mixture of multiple strategies

I have outlined the main investment strategies above; but there is nothing to stop you having multiple strategies at the same time. Many investors like to keep a pot of money for more speculative trades alongside other long-term investments.

The most important factor to consider is knowing which strategy you are following when making every single investment. A well-known phrase is 'a long-term investment is a short-term investment gone wrong'. That is the result of an investor failing to have an appropriate sell strategy and knowing when to cut their losses when something goes wrong or their goal is no longer achievable.

Investment strategies to be avoided

Buying shares that have fallen a long way on the belief that surely they will bounce back

There is no guarantee they will, and in all likelihood the company is on the way out. It happened to a friend of mine, who bought £10,000-worth of Northern Rock shares in 2008 when they were priced at 75p, having been over 1200p a year earlier. A few months later his money had gone forever.

Short-term plays on the Footsie

Again, just because the FTSE 100 has fallen two days in a row doesn't mean it will bounce back the next. You may say, "Yes it does, that happened yesterday." But that is no guarantee it will happen tomorrow.

If someone has told you about a sure-fire system for the FTSE, or any other index for that matter, don't believe them.

Early-stage oil or commodities plays

Getting in early in the one-in-a-thousand company that does become that next fast-growing central Asian energy giant sounds great in theory. But separating truth from fiction on the information you are getting on these companies is near impossible.

There are many other ways *not to invest*. Follow a combination of:

* don't be greedy

* don't invest in anything you don't understand

* if it looks like it is too good to be true, then it almost certainly is

* all mixed up with a dollop of common sense, should keep you on the straight and narrow.

19

CHOOSING A DIY INVESTMENT PLATFORM AND GETTING STARTED

We have talked about what an ISA, SIPP and dealing account can invest in and how much you can put in and take out in order to be as tax efficient as possible. Now let's talk about how you pick an investment platform in order to buy and sell assets and keep them safe.

DIY investment platforms can be assessed on a number of measures, but the most important, in my opinion, are functionality, service and price.

Functionality

A DIY investment platform is one that offers broadly the full range of investments covered in this book – namely equities, investment trusts, funds, gilts and corporate bonds. They will all offer an ISA, a SIPP and a dealing account.

Some of the following features may not be available on all DIY investment platforms, so they are worth investigating if they interest you:

- **Product range**. Does your preferred platform offer a Lifetime ISA or Junior ISAs? Does it offer a competitive Cash ISA or tools to help you make the most of your cash savings?

- **Joint accounts**. You may want to hold investments jointly with your spouse or partner for tax reasons. Not all platforms can cater for this.

- **Overseas shares**. Some may offer a limited range, some a full range and others may only allow investment in UK equities. All platforms will offer funds that can access overseas markets.

- **Mobile applications**. Most DIY platforms have some form of mobile offering, making it easier for you to deal on the go. The quality varies quite considerably.

- **Model portfolios and recommended funds lists**. These are very popular with people who are new to DIY investing. These model portfolios and recommended funds lists help you to put together a sensible portfolio in a matter of minutes. The inclusion of one or more of the funds offered by Woodford Investment Management on recommended funds lists has meant their reputation has taken a bit of a beating in the financial press over the last year or so. Provided the make-up of the funds list is subject to adequate ongoing due diligence and they're presented in an appropriate fashion I still believe they have a lot to offer. It would probably be a surprise to many to know that they remain as popular with savers as ever. I recall seeing a headline indicating that they had plummeted in popularity so checked the amount of web traffic to our own lists and found no reduction at all. However, please don't confuse the help you get choosing your investments with financial advice – where the adviser is providing you with a bespoke and tailored investment portfolio aligned to your risk appetite and objectives.

- **News and research**. All platforms will offer this to a greater or lesser degree, but some provide far more than others. Also, some platforms tend to focus on funds whereas others are more equity focused. You can normally sign up for information or newsletters even if you aren't a customer. Some investment platforms also publish their own magazines, including AJ Bell which publishes the weekly *Shares* magazine.

- **Regular investment/dividend reinvestment**. Not all platforms have a regular investment facility where you can invest cash held in your ISA, SIPP or dealing account into a specific fund or share on a regular basis, typically monthly. Also, you may want to check that your chosen platform can automatically reinvest your dividends received from equities or funds.

- **Linked accounts**. Can one person in the family manage all the family's accounts on the platform? I manage my SIPP, ISA and dealing account as well as my wife's ISA and my kids' ISAs, all via one login on the website and mobile application.

- **Reporting and data**. Does your platform offer secure messaging as an alternative to email? Does it offer performance reporting? Sophisticated DIY investors who actively deal in equities will often use Level 2 data to get detailed market information. Is this available? This information can be brought in separately if your DIY investment platform doesn't offer it. Is there a facility to enable your tax adviser to log in to your account on a read-only basis?

- **Certificated shares**. Few platforms nowadays allow you to sell shares where you hold a share certificate, and even fewer allow you to buy shares and hold a certificate.

- **Shareholder perks**. Not the benefit they used to be, but if you are interested in these, ask your platform whether or not they will give you access to them. Many won't due to the cumbersome administration and HMRC rules mean you won't be able to take advantage of the perks as a result of shares you hold in a pension.

Service

The assessment of the service standards of an investment platform can be quite subjective. All platforms put their best foot forward in marketing material, but you should treat client testimonials and awards logos littered over a platform's website with a healthy dose of scepticism.

There are several ways in which an investment platform's service proposition will affect your experience:

- **Website**. This is critical and will be your main interface with your investment platform. How easy is it to navigate? How intuitive is it to use? Is the 'search for investments' facility any good? Is the literature easy to understand?

- **Telephone and email support**. Try ringing them to ask a few questions to which you know the answer and see how knowledgeable and helpful the staff are. Try emailing and see how long it takes them to respond.

- **Online or offline**. Some platforms claim to offer a true online service, but at the first opportunity throw you into an offline, paper-based process. You should be able to apply for and pay money into a SIPP, ISA and a dealing account without printing off or signing any paper.

- **The independent view**. Try websites such as Feefo and Trustpilot to see what other customers think. Also, independent research houses such as Boring Money, Platforum and the lang cat prepare reports comparing the customer experience for different investment platforms.

Pricing

It is easiest to break charges down into product charges and investment charges. For product charges I mean the cost of establishing and running a SIPP, ISA or dealing account. For investment charges I mean the cost of buying, selling or holding an equity, fund, bond or any other investment covered in this book.

In order to assess which investment platform is the cheapest you will have to make some assumptions about the size of your accounts, what they are invested in – the split between shares and funds – and how often you buy/sell investments.

Hopefully, once you have chosen your investment platform you will be with them for many years to come, so consider how each of the above may change in the future. Your account values should increase as time marches on. Many DIY investors change their investment styles over time, so it is worth factoring this in when you are looking at charges.

Product or tax wrapper charges

You may see charges for some or all of the following:

- set-up or establishment
- annual administration
- contributions, subscriptions and transfer-in
- withdrawals and transfer-out.

These charges may be a monetary amount or *ad valorem*, which means a percentage of the value of the product. They may be a one-off charge or, where a regular charge, could be charged monthly, quarterly or annually, sometimes in advance and sometimes in arrears. Administration charges are normally also subject to VAT, so make sure you check whether the costs quoted are inclusive of VAT or are subject to VAT in addition.

These charges will normally be deducted directly out of your ISA, SIPP or dealing account. If you don't have sufficient cash to pay the charges then you will be given the chance to sell investments or inject some cash into your account. Failing that, the platform will sell your investments, normally on a last-in, first-out basis, to pay their charges.

SIPP-only charges

There is far more administration to be carried out on a SIPP than there is on an ISA or dealing account. SIPP-only charges are typically a fixed monetary amount and can include costs for:

- setting up an income drawdown pension, including paying any lump-sum benefits
- income drawdown administration
- purchasing an annuity with part, or all, of your SIPP
- transfer to, or from, another pension scheme in cash or in specie
- payment of benefits on death, or if your pension is to be split/shared following a divorce.

The above charges are normally a monetary amount rather than *ad valorem* and will attract VAT.

Investment charges

Dealing or investment commission – this may be a fixed fee per transaction, with the market level at about £10 per deal, or may be a percentage of the value of the investment being bought or sold. These are exempt from VAT.

The rate of dealing commission may vary depending on:

- **Whether online or via phone** – The latter is normally significantly dearer.

- **Whether in shares or funds** – Some platforms charge a lower dealing commission on funds.

- **Whether shares are listed in the UK or overseas** – The latter may be more expensive, and don't forget there will be a currency exchange cost as well.

- **How often you deal** – Many platforms have a frequent dealer commission rate. Typically, you will need to be dealing more than ten times a month to benefit.

- **Regular investments** – Lower dealing commission rates will normally apply for regular investments.

- **Dividend reinvestments** – Lower dealing commission rates will normally apply for dividend reinvestments.

- **Non-standard investments** – Those involving a paper application form will typically be subject to a higher dealing charge.

Custody charges

Your investment platform incurs a cost when buying and selling investments, but arguably the biggest cost to a platform is for holding the investments on your behalf. Custody charges are exempt from VAT and may be a fixed amount, *ad valorem*, or may not be charged at all.

Typically it costs an investment platform more to hold a fund on your behalf than it does to hold a share, so you will often find different levels of custody charges for funds and shares.

Other charges

Some platforms charge for corporate actions and some don't. This can be quite expensive if you have lots of equity holdings. Some charge for paper valuations, or additional copies of valuations, or consolidated tax vouchers, which are used for your tax return. If your platform's charges run to many pages, take this as a warning.

You will typically be charged for a telegraphic transfer of funds – for example if you want your cash transferred from your investment platform to you by same-day electronic transfer.

Cash rates

If you are likely to be holding large amounts of cash on your investment platform for long periods then the cash rate offered may be a factor in deciding which provider to go with. Though with the interest rates on cash having been low for a number of years, this hasn't been too much of a differentiator.

Interest rates are clearly displayed with the product and investment charges on all platforms' websites.

Some platforms have launched, or are in the process of launching, services which allow you to hold cash held in a range of deposit and fixed-term bank accounts alongside the other assets held via the platform.

How do I choose an investment platform?

Work out what you think your investment behaviour is likely to be over the next few years: how much money you will have, what will you be buying/selling, how often, how much cash will you have, and which tax wrappers will you use? Then use one of the research houses listed below to help you sift this down to a manageable number of platforms

– maybe two or three – and then carry out the wider research and due diligence described above.

One issue that has got more important over recent years – and is often overlooked by bargain-hunting DIY investors who are obsessed with price – is the financial strength of an investment platform and the sustainability of its pricing model.

It is easy to differentiate on price and it is a natural place to start when comparing investment platforms. However, you may be surprised to hear that very few investment platforms make any money. You can interpret this in a number of ways, but one very real risk of going with the cheapest, where that company is losing money, is that no sooner have you got your feet under their table than their prices will be increased.

The recent collapse of SVS Securities, a broker which had proven attractive with some savers because of its low headline charges, is another example of the need to look beyond a simple charges assessment. This book is not really the place to comment on the precise details of the collapse of SVS, but I think it is fair to say that the activities which forced the financial regulator to step in and effectively shut the firm down, may not have been necessary if it had operated a more sustainable charging model.

Moving investment platforms is not something you want to be doing every six months. Would you buy your clothes from the cheapest shop on the high street? Would you buy the cheapest car on the market? Were you burnt back in 2008 by chasing the highest interest rate only to find that it was the weakest banks and building societies that were offering these rates? It is about value as well as price, and don't underestimate the peace of mind that comes from knowing your money is held with a stable institution.

Do some financial due diligence on your preferred investment provider. Look at their accounts. See if they are making a profit.

There are several consultancies which publish reports comparing DIY investment platforms which you may find useful. These documents often include a comparison of charges, services, financial strength, reliability and range of investments. Platforum, Boring Money and the lang cat are good sources for this type of information.

Once you have chosen your investment platform, you are good to go. Choose which of the wrappers – SIPP, ISA, dealing account – you will use, fund them with cash and start building your portfolio.

A FINAL WORD

Now you have finished this book there is only one question you need to ask yourself: 'Am I a DIY investor?'

If the answer is no, then you need the help of a professional adviser and you can console yourself with the thought that at least you have avoided what could have been a costly mistake. You will also have a greater understanding of what advisers do for their money.

If the answer is yes, then I wish you good luck as you take control of your financial future. And don't forget, if you don't understand something, it is not your fault and DYOR.

Useful websites

- www.boringmoney.co.uk
- www.langcatfinancial.co.uk
- www.platforum.co.uk

INDEX

CPSIA information can be obtained
at www.ICGtesting.com
Printed in the USA
LVHW081446081021
699762LV00006B/6